HOLLYWOOD
THE GLAMOUR YEARS (1919-1941)

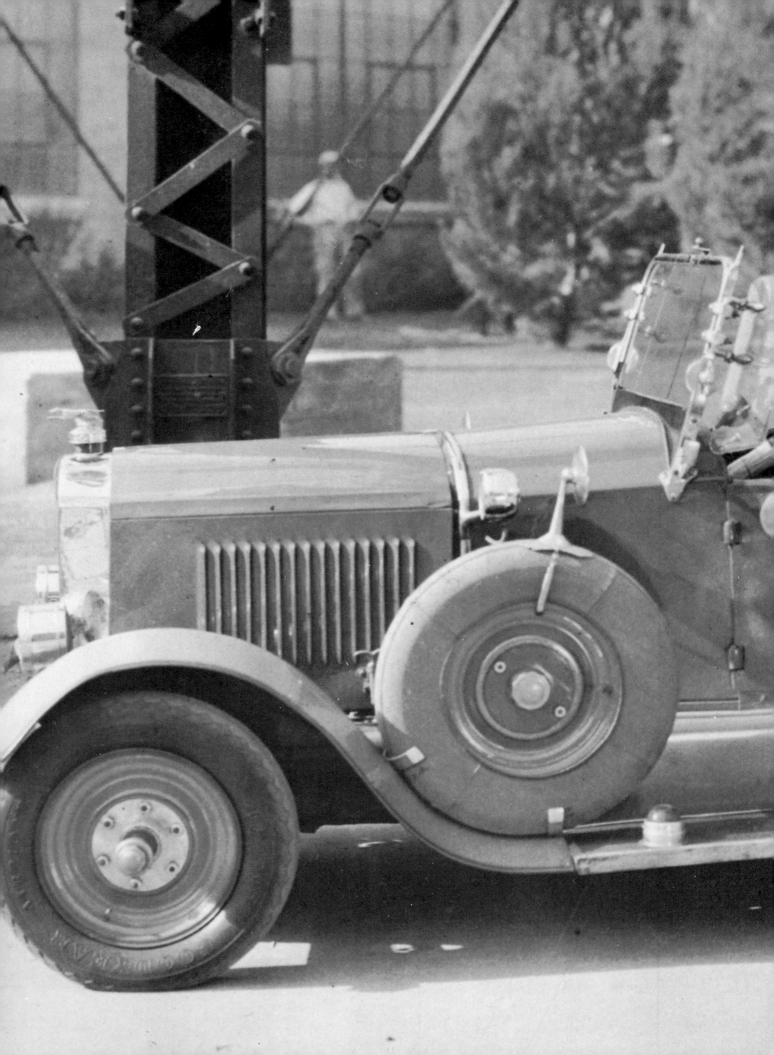

HOLLYWOOD
THE GLAMOUR YEARS (1919-1941)

ROBIN LANGLEY SOMMER

GALLERY BOOKS
An imprint of W.H. Smith Publishers Inc.
112 Madison Avenue
New York, New York 10016

A Bison Book

Published by Gallery Books
A Division of W H Smith Publishers Inc.
112 Madison Avenue
New York, New York 10016

Produced by
Bison Books Corp.
15 Sherwood Place
Greenwich, CT 06830

ISBN 0-8317-4519-3

Printed in Hong Kong

1 2 3 4 5 6 7 8 9 10

Page 1: Joan Crawford in a classic Glamour Years pose.
Pages 2-3: The ebullient Joan Blondell in 1931.
This page: The sprawling beach house built by William Randolph
Hearst for actress Marion Davies at Santa Monica.

CONTENTS

COLONIZING HOLLYWOOD

8

When the first filmmaker came to work in Los Angeles in 1908, Hollywood was a farming community of about 5000 people, populated mainly by transplanted Midwesterners who distrusted 'theater people' on principle. Saloons and theaters were outlawed, and profound distrust greeted the influx of moviemakers that began with Francis Boggs of the Selig Polyscope Company, who shot several scenes for *The Count of Monte Cristo* in Laguna Beach when bad winter weather in Chicago delayed the film.

Two years later, 15 young production companies were working in Hollywood at least part of the year, attracted by the West Coast's cheap land and labor, congenial climate, ready-made locations and distance from the New York-based Motion Picture Patents Trust.

New York City and New Jersey had nurtured the infant film industry under the aegis of inventor Thomas A Edison of the Edison Company, Albert Smith of Vitagraph, H N Marvin of Biograph and Frank Marion of Kalem. During the early Nickelodeon Age, when jerky one-reel dramas were shown in small-town storefronts and penny arcades, these men and half a dozen partners had a monopoly of film production, based on the patent laws. But when they sought to extend this monopoly to film distribution and exhibition, 'the fighting independents' of the distribution business – men like Carl

Laemmle and William Fox – rebelled. They refused either to sell out, or to pay the fee demanded by the controlling General Film Company: two dollars a week, 52 weeks a year.

When the General Film Trust cut off Carl Laemmle's supply of films, he went into the production business for himself as the Independent Motion-Picture Company (IMP). In so doing, he threw out the trust's second cardinal rule – that all movies, irrespective of quality, should be paid for at the rate of ten cents a foot. The door was open to competition, ushering in not only better films, but better prices for the good ones. The nascent film industry broke out of the mold that had

Previous pages: Hollywood in 1905 – a placid farming community transplanted almost bodily from the Middle West.

Top right: Dustin Farnum and Red Wing in the immensely successful film *The Squaw Man* (1914), shot by Cecil B De Mille in a rented Hollywood barn shared with the owner's horse. The picture triggered a wholesale exodus of the film industry from New York to Hollywood.

Below: The muddy track that was destined to become the glittering Sunset Strip – 1905.

defined it as a medium for 'immigrants, children, chambermaids and streetcar conductors.' The ground-breaking films of producer David Wark Griffith made audiences aware that they were no longer dealing with speechless copies of stage productions, but with a whole new art form. As President Woodrow Wilson said after viewing Griffith's epic *Birth of a Nation* in 1915, 'It is like writing history with lightning.'

Griffith's powerful drama of the Civil War and Reconstruction South caused riots and protests, but it was not ignored. The fact that it had been made on the West Coast could only enhance California's increasing appeal to filmmakers – some of whom had been subject to physical attacks as a result of their defiance of the Trust. After Cecil B De Mille filmed *The Squaw Man* in a rented Hollywood barn in 1913, the exodus from New York was on. A steady stream of ambitious young producers, players and technicians began migrating into the Los Angeles area before the United States entered World War I. Their numbers were swelled by film personnel from Europe who came upon hard times during the war years. By 1920, 36,000 people were living in Hollywood – most of them members of the film colony who found lodgings as best they could in a hostile environment. Boardinghouses posted signs saying *No Dogs and No Actors*. The factory-like studios were resented as eyesores by conservative locals, and the new movie people were referred to as 'gypsies.' The general middle-class prejudice against 'big-city' folk was increased by the fact that most of the independent filmmakers were either foreign-born or Jewish – often both.

Ambitious entrepreneurs could not help but be attracted into the new film industry. Samuel Goldfish (who became Samuel Goldwyn) started out as a glove salesman in Chicago. Then he formed a partnership with Jesse Lasky, a vaudeville musician, and New York actor-turned-manager Cecil B De

Mille. Goldfish purchased the rights to a Western novel that became *The Squaw Man* – the wildly successful motion picture that was the first full-length movie made in Hollywood. Other independents – Adolph Zukor, Carl Laemmle, Marcus Loew, William Fox – challenged the Trust and ultimately defeated it in the courts. They founded four of the companies that have dominated the industry for 75 years: Paramount, Universal, Loew's-MGM and Fox (which would merge with Twentieth Century Pictures).

As long as New York remained the center of filmmaking, Broadway actors dominated the movies. The 10-minute 'flickers' shown to working-class audiences in store-front theaters were looked down upon by serious actors, but as the independents began paying more and more money, the movies' status increased. After World War I, when Euro-

Above: Hollywood's first studio, home of the Christie and Nestor Comedies, at Sunset and Gower Street. Even in 1915, it was clear that the automobile had a future in California.

Below: Three of the industry's pathfinders, from left, director D W Griffith, independent producer Carl Laemmle Jr and theater-chain owner Sid Grauman.

Above: Universal Pictures adopted the popular Spanish style for its impressive North Hollywood studio, seen here on a postcard inscribed 'Ate lunch at Universal Studio Cafe – with the stars'.

Below: Independent filmmakers Adolph Zukor (left) and Marcus Loew were in the forefront of the industry as the founders of Paramount and Loew's-MGM, when production and distribution went hand in hand.

pean artists emigrated to Hollywood, film-making became even more respectable. Directors like Ernst Lubitsch, Erich von Stroheim and F W Murnau brought their finely honed skills to America. The best European designers and craftsmen flocked to the West Coast.

Of course, there was opposition to the new medium, and controversy about the movies' effect on traditional values. As early as 1907, the *Chicago Tribune* complained that the movies were 'without a redeeming feature to warrant their existence . . . ministering to the lowest passions of childhood.' Audiences disagreed.

Before World War I disrupted European filmmaking, feature-length films had been imported by ambitious showmen and pre-sented in legitimate theaters. They attracted a more sophisticated group than the one- and two-reel domestic products. In 1913 the first movie palace was built in New York City. During the 1910s and 1920s, even more luxurious 'cathedrals of the motion picture' sprang up all over the country. Most seated several thousand patrons and boasted elaborate drapery, crystal-and-gold chandeliers, Oriental motifs, huge Wurlitzer organs, statues of Mayan gods and other exotica. At the Fifth Avenue Theatre in Seattle, the ceiling replicated the vault in the Imperial Throne Room of the Forbidden City of Peking. Radio City Music Hall, the world's biggest theater, had a stage so large that front-row patrons couldn't see all of it, and not one but three consoles for its incomparable theater organ. It was all part of the fantasy. As psychologist Bruno Bettelheim would recall decades later: 'The moviehouses to which I went as a youth were true pleasure domes, very different from those of today. As soon as one entered these old dream palaces, one felt transposed to another world. Inside, there were nooks and crannies and boxes with heavy curtains which suggested privacy and intimacy. Here one could escape the watchful scrutiny of one's parents and all other adults, and do nothing constructive whatsoever – but daydream.'

Cartoonist Jules Feiffer summed it up when he said of his childhood, 'Not for a moment did I believe that I was meant to live in the Bronx. I was not meant to be poor. A terrible mistake had been made. At four and a half, I learned that only movies could correct it.'

Ultimately, the independents defeated the Trust by the process of intuition. They grasped the fact that the pioneer filmmakers had underestimated the potential of the industry. The Trust had refused to reveal the identity of its players, assuming (correctly) that famous players would demand bigger salaries. But the public was not to be fobbed off indefinitely with 'the Biograph girl' or 'the girl with the golden curls.' It wanted to know the identities of the stars it idolized, and the independents were prepared to meet this demand. They identified their stars by name, provided details on their personal lives (both real and spurious) and paid the higher salaries that resulted from this publicity. The star system that prevailed when the Glamour Years began was created and maintained by the movie-going public.

By 1919 Hollywood had already become the world capital of motion-picture production. It produced four out of every five movies and constituted America's fifth largest industry, grossing over $700 million a year. Many of the early silent-movie stars are

scarcely remembered now – John Bunny, for example, was an incredibly popular comedian of the 1910s in a series of one-reelers. People named their children for him. Francis X Bushman kept his marriage to Beverly Bayne a secret when they played screen lovers in *Romeo and Juliet* (1916), so as not to disillusion their fans. But when the secret leaked out, along with evidence of bigamy, Bushman's career foundered. The lesson was not lost on Hollywood, which sought to present its stars as unattached (and therefore attainable if only in daydreams), no matter what their marital status. But publicists had to tread a fine line between availability and promiscuity. Any hint of scandal was box-office poison.

Some of the early silent stars became legends in their own time, like Norma Talmadge, who was a beautiful leading lady at Vitagraph in her teens. Her sister Constance was a featured player with the Griffith company. The Gish sisters, Lillian and Dorothy, came to Los Angeles in 1914 for Lillian's role as Elsie Stoneman in *The Birth of a Nation* (1915). (Later, Lillian Gish would recall that they had rented a five-room apartment on Hope Street 'because it was cheap and I could ride the streetcar back and forth to the studio.')

Moviemakers also turned to New York for

established stage players to meet the ever-growing demands of film production. Opera star Geraldine Farrar and matinee idol Wallace Reid made a fiery couple in Cecil B De Mille's elaborate *Carmen* (1915). Other crossovers from the legitimate theater, including Russian-born Alla Nazimova, enjoyed great popularity – provided they did not play roles that were too highbrow. However, many stage-trained actors could not meet the test of the silent screen. Deprived of their voices, they fell back on exaggerated pantomimed effects that the camera magnified to the point of laughability. Hollywood photoplayers who had dreaded the invasion of big-name Broadway professionals were relieved to find out that Adolph Zukor's series of 'Famous Players in Famous Plays' was a resounding flop. The public stoutly rejected stagey performers like opera star Mary Garden, whom they considered hams. Garden's statuesque poses and frozen reactions led one critic to describe her film debut as 'a close approach to a motionless motion picture.' Instead, audiences demanded established favorites in their familiar roles: spunky 'Little Mary' Pickford; seductive Theda Bara; Charlie Chaplin, 'the Little Fellow'; and the dashing Douglas Fairbanks. Pioneer screenwriter Anita Loos, the author of *Gentlemen Prefer Blondes*, tells the story of how Douglas Fairbanks Sr became a movie star in the film comedy *His Picture in the Papers*, which the Griffith studio produced as a trial balloon in 1915. It is a case study in the star system.

Fairbanks had been imported from Broadway, where he was enjoying a modest success in light comedy roles. However, his first few

Above: Director Maurice Tourneur confers with Mary Pickford during the filming of *Poor Little Rich Girl* (1917). Lucien Andriot mans the camera. Pickford's popularity was so great that she could command six-figure salaries during the early Glamour Years.

Left: The incomparable Lillian Gish, who made her Hollywood debut in D W Griffith's *Birth of a Nation* (1915). She had been working with Biograph in New York since 1912.

pictures made little impression, and Griffith was preparing to drop his option, while the young actor himself was increasingly homesick for New York. Loos prepared a screenplay with humorous subtitles – much more extensive than usual – that starred Fairbanks in a spoof of the wealthy nearby community of Pasadena. She and her future husband, director John Emerson, also left in the spontaneous horseplay improvised by the high-spirited young actor on the set. When the picture reached New York, it was rushed to the Roxy Theatre, where showman S L 'Roxy' Rothafel complained bitterly, because Fairbanks was almost unknown. However, the Exchange had failed to deliver his scheduled feature film and he had to use *His Picture in the Papers*. Roxy puffed up to the stage and apologized to the audience, promising to pull the picture as soon as the expected feature arrived.

When the Fairbanks comedy began to roll, roars of laughter greeted the first subtitle. They increased to a gale as the film continued. Halfway through the picture, the missing feature arrived, and Roxy made his way back to the stage and lifted his hand to stop the show. '"Listen, children, the regular film just got here. Do you want me to yank Doug Fairbanks?" "No! No! No!" came a reply that sounded like thunder. The picture continued to a hilarious end, by which time Doug Fairbanks had put an entire audience permanently into his pocket.'

Later, of course, the athletic Fairbanks became even more popular as the star of such

Above: Mary Pickford and colleagues clown on the set of *Rosita* (1923), in which 'America's Sweetheart' played a Spanish street singer. Behind Pickford is screenwriter Edward Knoblock, helping to hold up the ever-athletic Douglas Fairbanks, whose other prop is the German director Ernst Lubitsch.

Right: Popular Keystone Comedy star Chester Conklin is about to be drenched in one of Mack Sennett's popular slapstick comedies (1915).

swashbucklers as *The Thief of Bagdad* (1924) and other vehicles in which he performed his own hair-raising stunts, swinging into a scene on ropes and descending the length of a velvet curtain by cutting it with his outthrust sword. (Even at home, Fairbanks' bemused guests were treated to a running exhibition of handstands, dives and broad jumps.)

Other personalities were in equal demand by the public, which knew what it wanted, including Mack Sennett comedies with bathing beauties, Keystone Kops and Mabel Normand, the gifted comedienne. (Sennett endeared himself to staid long-time residents of Hollywood by spreading oil at street intersections and filming the skids as part of his comedies.) The public also wanted William S Hart playing the good bad guy in the cinematic Wild West pioneered by 'Bronco Billy' Anderson's Essanay productions. It demanded, and got, action-packed serials that bridged the awkward transition from two-reelers to features and confirmed the movie-going addiction of a nation.

The first serial was produced by the Edison Company in 1912 to satisfy the growing demand for competitive product. The popular newspaper *McClure's Ladies World* was then running an adventure-story series called 'What Happened to Mary?' and Edison used it as the basis for several short films. The success of the format, which starred Mary Fuller as the Little Orphan Annie-type heroine, was immediate, and Edison rushed additional melodramas into production:

Mary in Stageland, A Clue to Her Parentage and *The High Tide of Misfortune.* The following year, Kathlyn Williams and Tom Santschi made the first action-oriented serial, entitled *The Adventures of Kathlyn.* The beautiful heroine was pursued by sundry villains and wild animals as she tried to lay claim to a title she had inherited in India. This improbable scenario was a great success, and in 1914 an even more appealing heroine appeared in the form of Pearl White, who played the title role in 20 episodes of *The Perils of Pauline.* The films were amateurishly directed and full of inconsistencies, but the public took Pearl to its heart and made her the screen's major serial heroine. She was soon copied by Helen Holmes, Helen Gibson and Ruth Roland, who made hundreds of episodic cliffhangers.

Above: Douglas Fairbanks gets ready to launch himself through space in his trademark daredevil leap. Fairbanks did all his own stunts in his films.

Bottom left: Comedienne Mabel Normand and producer Mack Sennett starred together in numerous Keystone Comedies of the early Glamour Years. They were romantically involved off-screen as well.

Below: Serial star Pearl White registers dismay as only she could in William Fox's *Beyond Price* (1916).

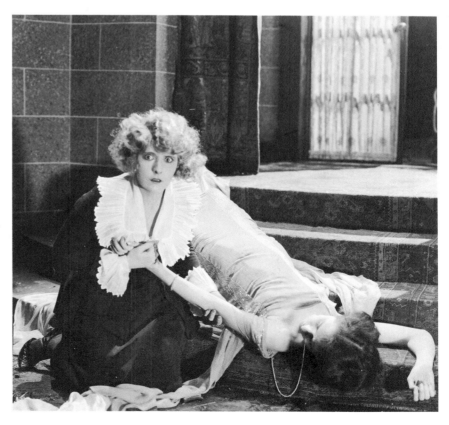

By the mid-1910s, known actors and actresses were demanding and getting $250 to $500 a week – a far cry from the five to ten dollars a week (and no screen credit) offered to the first film players at the turn of the century. A few stars like Mary Pickford commanded salaries in the hundreds of thousands. The basis was what film historians Arthur Mayer and Richard Griffith have called 'something indefinable and uniquely cinematic' – a quality that audiences could identify with or admire. Personality was at the heart of it, and no amount of technique or even physical beauty could compensate for its absence.

The inevitable result of the star system was that the most popular performers increased their salary demands beyond what even the most successful studios could – or would – pay. In 1919 four of the biggest names in Hollywood formed United Artists to produce and distribute their own pictures: Douglas Fairbanks, Charlie Chaplin, Mary Pickford and D W Griffith. In the mid-1920s, they were joined by producer Joseph M Schenck, who brought in Norma and Con-

stance Talmadge, Gloria Swanson, John
Barrymore and Buster Keaton.

As the prestige and popularity of the
movies increased, the town of Hollywood
took a brighter view of the 'gypsies' who had
encamped in its midst. There was a shift away
from the mood described by director Allan
Dwan, who recalled that in the early days 'If
we walked in the streets with our cameras,
they hid their girls under the beds, closed
doors and windows and shied away.' Now
that the movies had become the country's
leading entertainment medium, the moviemakers were regarded with more tolerance.
The film community still had its complaints
about Hollywood, though. It remained a dry
town, and entertainers who were used to
New York and Chicago found it slow going.

When the Glamour Years began, movie
stars who had rented modest apartments and
worked seven days a week for twelve hours a
day were ready to cut loose and spend some
of their hard-earned money. It was clear by
now that the movies were no passing novelty
– that their new-found affluence would not
evaporate with the passing of a fad. But what

to do for entertainment among the bean and
poppy fields, where the occasional coyote
still rambled through town? There was Craw-
ston's Pasadena Ostrich Farm and Chute's
Amusement Park at Main and Washington
Streets – not exactly Delmonico's. On a
brighter note, there was horseracing at Ascot
Park, in south central Los Angeles, where one
could also buy a drink. Pasadena's annual
Tournament of Roses offered football games
and chariot races. The heavy-weight fights at
the Vernon Arena might feature champion
Jim Jeffries, and race-car driver Barney
Oldfield operated the Western Athletic Club,
which also sponsored prize fights on Satur-
day nights. By the 1920s, Friday night fights
at the Hollywood Legion Stadium would be a
popular outing.

The Hollywood Hotel's Thursday night
gatherings had already become the focal point
of the film colony's local social life. Pro-
prietress Mira Hershey, of the chocolate-
making family, kept a watchful eye on the
high-spirited movie set in the imposing
Mission-Moorish-style hostelry, which had
opened in 1903 after tourists began to discover California.

The Thursday-night dances were re-
strained affairs, featuring, as Anita Loos recalled it, 'a string quartet of lady musicians
who could be counted on for refined selections. No Charlestons, no Bunny Hops . . .
While poor Miss Hershey watched from the
sidelines, jittering with affront, those movie
actors purposefully made a sport of being
caught in "lewd" dancing and getting ordered
off the floor.' Wine and liquor were regularly
smuggled into the dining room. After learning that some actors were climbing through
the ground-floor bedroom windows to visit
their lady friends, Miss Hershey planted large
cacti under each sill (and checked regularly to
be sure that no amorous gentleman had dug
one up).

Downtown Los Angeles had more diver-
sions to offer, and many movie people rented
rooms or apartments there. Some stayed at
the Alexandria Hotel at Spring and Eighth
Streets. There producers, directors and actors
rendezvoused in the ornate lobby, with its
marble columns and potted palms. The bar
offered free sandwiches as well as cocktails,
which made it a natural gathering place for
out-of-work actors looking for contacts. It
was here that Rudolph Valentino got the
break that put him into the movies. Jack
Warner lived at the Alexandria for several
years, and restaurateur Herbert Somborn
(who would soon open his first Brown Derby
nearby) met Mack Sennett bathing beauty
Gloria Swanson in the hotel's dining room.
They were married soon afterward.

Deals were made over food and drinks all

Right: The Red Car trolley tied Hollywood to metropolitan Los Angeles and brought tourists out to stare at the fast-growing studios and their exotic stars.

Below: The angular Alexandria Hotel, at Spring and Eighth Streets in downtown Los Angeles, was a professional and social center for the film community. Newcomers from the East Coast often made extended stays here until they found work and housing.

along Spring Street, which began to advertise itself as the Great White Way West. The biggest establishment was the Imperial Cafe, which ran a full block between Spring and Broadway. Its balcony overlooked a colorful cross-section of Los Angeles night life – bars, dance halls, theaters and movie houses. Al Levy's, at Third and Main, featured a push-cart on its roof – a memento of the days when its owner had vended oysters in front of theaters before he arrived on the great Gold Coast. Studio technicians hung out at the Hoffman Bar, and McKee's Restaurant included a floor show. However, Los Angeles city ordinances of the day were restrictive about mixing dancing and liquor, so many film-colony members went farther afield for their social life.

The popular Vernon County Club – an unpretentious-looking roadhouse in the middle of surrounding beet fields – was Hollywood's first real nightclub. But then Vernon (an independent town that scoffed at blue laws) was wide open compared to Los Angeles. Sports promoter Jack Doyle had opened a lively watering hole there, and Indiana-born Baron Long followed his example when he established the Vernon Country Club in 1912. It enjoyed a great success until it burned to the ground in 1929.

The Vernon reportedly introduced jazz to Southern California, and its liberal drinking policy attracted the biggest names in early

Hollywood. Roscoe 'Fatty' Arbuckle (who would later open a club of his own), Mary Pickford, America's Sweetheart (called by her studio the Bank of America's Sweetheart), Wallace Reid, D W Griffith and a host of other personalities converged on isolated Vernon and made the rafters ring. The flamboyant cowboy actor Tom Mix once drove his car right into the club and ordered drinks for the house. Rudolph Valentino worked there as a tango dancer before he became an idol of the silent screen. 'The Baron' seemed immune to prosecution for the gambling that went on in the club's many private rooms. It was here that the integration of floor show, dancing, chorus girls and orchestra was introduced – a combination that became a nightclub standard.

Not far from the Vernon Country Club was another Baron Long establishment, the popular Ship Café, built on a pier in Venice-by-the-Sea. It was a combination hotel and restaurant with an elaborate menu and popular dancing contests, culminating in the feverish New Year's Eve celebrations that would become a fixture of Hollywood night life. The stationary 'ship' had been christened the *Cabrillo*, and its Spanish-galleon motif included the staff, who were dressed to re-semble (loosely) sixteenth-century naval officers. Comedian Buster Keaton once jumped out of a porthole there in a well-publicized attempt to 'escape' his many fans.

Other beach cities offered diverse attractions to the far-ranging film community. Fraser's Million-Dollar Pier in Ocean Park had roller coasters, theaters, gaudy shows, even opium dens. The nearby Café Nat Goodwin, built on a private pier at the foot of Hollister Avenue, was a glamourous cabaret frequented by such luminaries as Charlie Chaplin and Mabel Normand. Festooned with electric lights, it was advertised as 'the most beautiful cafe over-the-sea in the world' and boasted a roof garden, a ballroom and parking space for 350 racy roadsters. The proprietor was nicknamed 'Marrying Nat' (he set an early Hollywood record with eight marriages) and had been a popular stage comedian before he branched off into the cabaret business. Chaplin, who lived in Santa Monica at this time, was a friend and admirer of the enterprising restauranteur.

Public dancing may have been outlawed in Hollywood, but it was wildly popular along the coast. Ballrooms like the Egyptian, the Venice and the Three O'Clock sponsored 'movie nights' as a showcase for studio talent,

Fraser's Million-Dollar Pier in Ocean Park had a multitude of gaudy attractions that drew throngs of pleasure-bent visitors from Hollywood, where local ordinances were stricter.

and enormous crowds packed into these popular jazz emporiums. Culver City's outdoor Danceland had parking for 3000 cars (California led the way into the automotive age) and a dance floor so large that MGM used it as the set for the Circus Maximus in *Ben Hur* (1925). The Cinderella Roof Ballroom was another popular rendezvous for Hollywood merry-makers.

Baron Long's third successful enterprise was the Sunset Inn, below the bluffs of Santa Monica, where Abe Lyman's band played for dance contests and 'carnival nights' brought in stars like Bebe Daniels and Colleen Moore to dance till closing. When Eddie Brandstatter and Mike Lyman took over at the Sunset Inn, Thursday became the big night – the 'Fillum Fotoplayer Food Festival,' when big-name guests were the main attraction and special dishes were named in honor of reigning stars.

When World War I ended in 1919, the prewar boom in Los Angeles oil and real-estate was eclipsed by the new rush into the city and its suburbs, including Hollywood. The attraction was increased by the fact that millions had seen the attractive bungalows and tree-shaded streets in the backgrounds of countless movies. Many of the new arrivals were aspiring film stars, lured by ads that promised fame and money to future 'photoplayers.' They would not be deterred by rejection, nor by the sign eventually posted outside the Central Casting Office on Western Avenue: 'DON'T TRY TO BECOME AN ACTOR. FOR EVERY ONE WE EMPLOY, WE TURN AWAY A THOUSAND.' But non-acting jobs in film production were plentiful. So were jobs in manufacturing and oil production. During the 1920s, the area's population would more than double, and the film community would generate more night life, more glamour, more scandal and more money than southern California – or almost anyplace else – had dreamed of since the search for El Dorado.

Left: Bewigged and costumed extras line up at the Goldwyn Studios in 1920. Undeterred by low pay and rejection, almost everyone wanted to be in the movies – busboys, bellhops, bartenders and high-school beauty queens.

Below: The spacious main dining room at Nat Goodwin's Cafe, built on a pier over the Pacific at Santa Monica. It was one of the most-frequented seaside resorts.

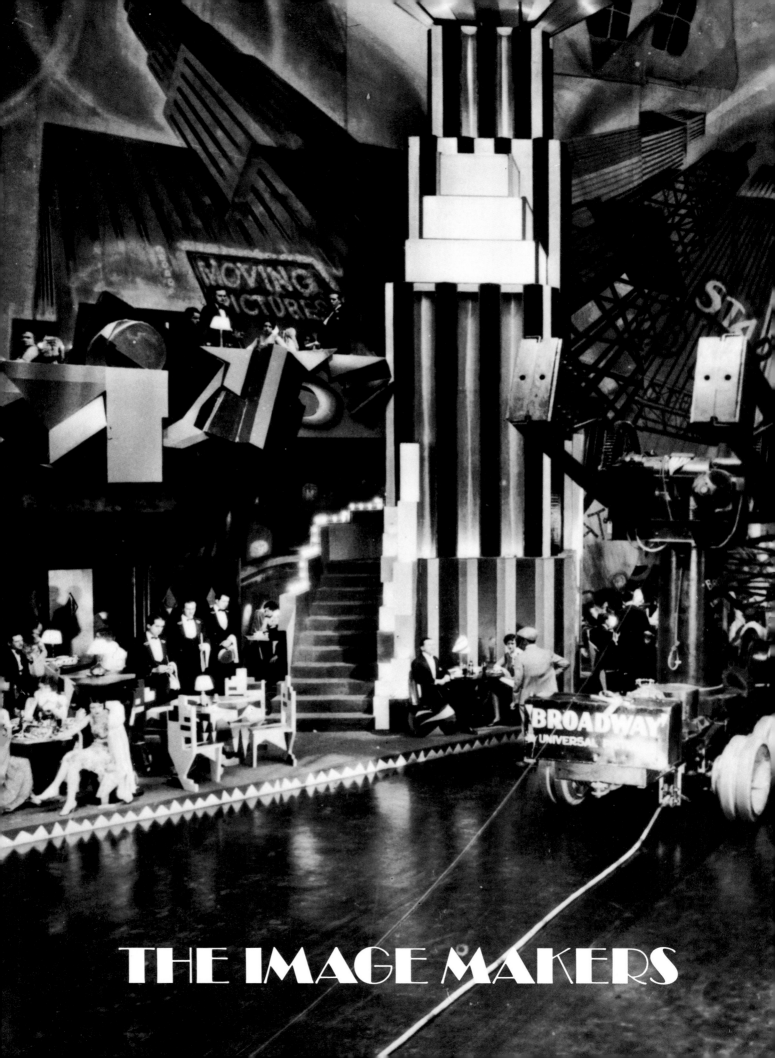

THE IMAGE MAKERS

The men who dominated the industrial development of the movies were, almost without exception, immigrants who learned to survive in a hard school. Adolph Zukor had come to America from Hungary in 1888, with $40 sewed into the lining of his suit. Carl Laemmle had emigrated from Germany four years before Zukor and worked at many menial jobs until he accumulated the small sum that was needed to buy a nickelodeon or penny arcade at the turn of the century. William Fox peddled blacking in his early childhood to help support his family after their arrival from Hungary. Louis B Mayer, born in Minsk, Poland, was a beachcomber and scrap dealer when he first came to the New World. The Warner Brothers – Harry, Abe, Same and Jack – were the sons of a Polish cobbler. Samuel Goldwyn (born Goldfish) was a Midwestern glove salesman who had immigrated from Poland at the age of 11. And Marcus Loew had sold newspapers and then worked in the fur trade before he and his partners set up a vaudeville chain that established a million-dollar movie sideline in the mid-1910s.

The modest early investments these men had made in the future of mass entertainment were already consolidating into valuable sources of income before the defeat of the Patent Trust's effort to monopolize the movie industry. Universal was founded by Carl Laemmle and partners in 1912, and Adolph Zukor's famous Players merged with Jesse Lasky's company to form Paramount Pictures in 1914. Metro Pictures was founded in 1915 by Louis B Mayer, Richard Rowland and several partners. Sam Goldwyn left

Previous pages: Films like Universal's *Broadway*, with its lavish Paradise Night Club set, fueled Hollywood's reputation for glamour at any cost.

Top right: Janet Gaynor prepares to crash Paramount's imposing gate in *A Star is Born* (1937).

Below: Members of the Pickford Company dine al fresco on location: from left, director Al Green; Jack Pickford, whose brief career was marred by alcoholism and three unhappy marriages; and his sister Mary, the first movie star. Adolph Zukor, head of Famous Players, gave Pickford her own company as an inducement to join his troupe in the 1910s.

Zukor to form the Goldwyn Company. The Warner brothers expanded from distribution into production on the strength of a 1918 picture entitled *My Four Years in Germany* (although they lacked the money and muscle of the larger studios for many years to come).

The movie industry slumped briefly after World War I, when its backlog of war movies fell out of favor and European markets embargoed American films. But the prosperity of the national postwar economy salvaged the new film capital of Hollywood, as investors came forward in droves to buy or back theaters. They included those who had profited hugely from the war, barkeepers put out of business by Prohibition, bankers and financiers. Theater owners outdid each other in building bigger and more elaborate movie palaces, while the producers cranked up their cameras again. When Mary Pickford left Adolph Zukor for United Artists in 1919, her former employer offered her a quarter of a million dollars to retire from the screen for the next five years. Then Famous Players-Lasky set up Mary Miles Minter as a rival to America's Sweetheart, while a consortium of major producers and directors that included William Ince, Mack Sennett, King Vidor and Allan Dwan formed Associated Producers. In 1921 this group merged with First National as Associated First National.

Wall Street began to take a serious interest in the movies. New capital financed a resurgence of American films in European markets and the pirating of European talent to enrich the American industry. The early informal methods by which movies were improvised as they went along, often without a script, were tightened up. Supervisors were put in charge of every picture, with control over budget, script, casting and final editing. The top studios began to produce a major feature almost every week, which they distributed to their own theaters through their own exchanges. Paramount had studios not only in Hollywood, but in New York, London, Paris and Berlin. Columbia, Universal and Warner Bros. sought to match the pace set by the major producers. A host of hopeful independent producers ground out low-budget comedies and Westerns for small-town and small-theater audiences.

The movies had been deplored by various moralists almost since they began. But in the early 1920s, censorship became an issue as a result of several factors. One was pointed out by Anita Loos. 'By this time the stars were moving out of the Hollywood Hotel and beginning to live in their own private homes with servants, most of whom were their peers in everything but sex appeal – which pinpoints the reason for the film capital's mass

misbehavior. To place in the limelight a great number of people who ordinarily would be chambermaids and chauffeurs, give them unlimited power and instant wealth, is bound to produce a lively and diverting result.'

The second factor was the backlash of several scandals that rocked Hollywood in the early 1920s, most notably the death of starlet Virginia Rappe after a weekend drink-

Above: The four Warner brothers were struggling to keep their studio afloat until they gambled on the new Vitaphone sound process in the mid-1920s.

Below: The Christie Comedy Company on location in 1917.

ing party at a San Francisco hotel. Fatty
Arbuckle was arrested and charged with
manslaughter, and prurient speculation about
what had gone on between the popular
comedian and the young girl destroyed the
actor's career, even though he was acquitted
of the charge after several trials. Mary Miles
Minter was implicated in the unsolved
murder of director William Desmond Taylor
by love letters found in his possession, and
her chance to become the second Mary Pickford vanished in the scandal. Mabel Normand's name was also linked to Taylor's,
and rumors of narcotic addiction plagued her
after popular actor Wallace Reid died as a
result of drug abuse. The public demanded
reform and alarmed studio heads, eager to
avoid outside censorship, hired President
Harding's Postmaster General, Will Hays, to
police the industry from within. For the next
23 years, the Hays Office sought to impose its
standards of propriety on the filmmakers,
who regularly defied its restrictive code and
the sanctions of local communities. As director Raoul Walsh would recall years later:
'Everybody had battles with the censors . . .
A kiss could only last three seconds. You
weren't allowed to take any love scene if there
was a bed visible, even if it was a mile away
down the road. Every state had its own censors and Pennsylvania was the toughest.
Whenever anybody took a scene that was the
least bit off, everybody would yell: "It won't
be shown in Pennsylvania!" But we battled
on. Sometimes we'd take maybe six or seven
risqué scenes, hoping they'd leave two.'
Strictures were restated in the industry's
more rigorous 1930 Production Code, which
followed upon the formation of the Roman
Catholic Legion of Decency by the American

Catholic bishops. When 10 million Catholics
were asked to pledge that they would boycott
movies that 'offend decency and Christian
morality,' moviemakers took notice.

In the middle 1920s, a series of mergers had
consolidated power in the movie industry.
Marcus Loew united Goldwyn with Louis B
Mayer's Metro Studio and took in Cosmopolitan Pictures, which had been formed by
William Randolph Hearst to produce the
pictures of Marion Davies after he removed
her from the Ziegfeld chorus line. Mayer's
name was included in the title of the organization that became known as MGM.

The Famous Players Theatres were combined with the Balaban and Katz vaudeville
circuits to form Public Theatres – a feint at
divorcing Paramount's production activities
from its distribution network to avoid
Federal Trade Commission complaints about
monopoly. Other chains were combined to
form the Stanley Company of America. The
independent theater owner was out of the
picture.

In 1914 the first of the great Wurlitzer
organs had been installed in a Paterson, New
Jersey, cinema. The Mark Strand Theatre in
New York City awed patrons with its luxury
and elegance, until it was eclipsed in 1927 by
Rothafel's Roxy Theatre, with its 'Gothic
form, renaissance detail and Moorish atmosphere.' But competition was fierce: the
Capitol, Loew's State, the Paramount, Radio
City Music Hall and the Grauman theaters all
entered the contest for movie palace of the
decade during the 1920s. The nickelodeon
was a fading memory, as tickets for a Griffith
premiere rose to three and five dollars apiece.

As the United States became increasingly
urban, sophisticated, even cynical in the years

Top left: Roscoe Arbuckle is arraigned on first-degree murder charges in a San Francisco courtroom – 12 September 1921.

Above: Former Postmaster General Will Hays is introduced to Hollywood at the Lasky Studios on Vine Street. The Hays Office would seek to police the movie industry from within, as an alternative to outside censorship.

Left: The text of the rigorous 1930 Production Code that governed what Hollywood could and couldn't show on screen for over 30 years.

TEXT OF THE PRODUCTION CODE

tent of the Code appear in two parts—first, a working abstract of the Code which has been widely accepted as the complete Code, and, second, the Code proper, which has been referred to as "Reasons Supporting a Code".

GENERAL PRINCIPLES

1. No picture shall be produced which will lower the moral standards of those who see it. Hence the sympathy of the audience should never be thrown to the side of crime, wrong-doing, evil or sin.
2. Correct standards of life, subject only to the requirements of drama and entertainment, shall be presented.
3. Law, natural or human, shall not be ridiculed, nor shall sympathy be created for its violation.

PARTICULAR APPLICATIONS

I. CRIMES AGAINST THE LAW

These shall never be presented in such a way as to throw sympathy with the crime as against law and justice or to inspire others with a desire for imitation.

1. **Murder**
   a. The technique of murder must be presented in a way that will not inspire imitation.
   b. Brutal killings are not to be presented in detail.
   c. Revenge in modern times shall not be justified.
2. **Methods of crime** should not be explicitly presented.
   a. Theft, robbery, safe-cracking and dynamiting of trains, mines, buildings, etc., should not be detailed in method.
   b. Arson must be subject to the same safeguards.
   c. The use of firearms should be restricted to essentials.
   d. Methods of smuggling should not be presented.
3. **Illegal drug traffic** must never be presented.
4. **The use of liquor** in American life, when not required by the plot or for proper characterization, will not be shown.

II. SEX

The sanctity of the institution of marriage and the home shall be upheld. Pictures shall not infer that low forms of sex relationship are the accepted or common thing.

1. **Adultery,** sometimes necessary plot material, must not be explicitly treated, or justified, or presented attractively.
2. **Scenes of passion**
   a. They should not be introduced when not essential to the plot.
   b. Excessive and lustful kissing, lustful embraces, suggestive postures and gestures, are not to be shown.
   c. In general, passion should so be treated that these scenes do not

stimulate the lower and baser element.
3. **Seduction or rape**
   a. They should never be more than suggested, and only when essential for the plot, and even then never shown by explicit method.
   b. They are never the proper subject for comedy.
4. **Sex perversion** or any inference to it is forbidden.
5. **White slavery** shall not be treated.
6. **Miscegenation** (sex relationships between the white and black races) is forbidden.
7. **Sex hygiene** and venereal diseases are not subjects for motion pictures.
8. Scenes of **actual child birth,** in fact or in silhouette, are never to be presented.
9. **Children's sex organs** are never to be exposed.

III. VULGARITY

The treatment of low, disgusting, unpleasant, though not necessarily evil, subjects should be subject always to the dictates of good taste and a regard for the sensibilities of the audience.

IV. OBSCENITY

Obscenity in word, gesture, reference, song, joke, or by suggestion (even when likely to be understood only by part of the audience) is forbidden.

V. PROFANITY

Pointed profanity (this includes the words: God, Lord, Jesus, Christ—unless used reverently—Hell, S.O.B., damn, Gawd), or every other profane or vulgar expression however used, is forbidden.

VI. COSTUME

1. **Complete nudity** is never permitted. This includes nudity in fact or in silhouette, or any lecherous or licentious notice thereof by other characters in the picture.
2. **Undressing scenes** should be avoided, and never used save where essential to the plot.

3. **Indecent or undue exposure** is forbidden.
4. **Dancing costumes** intended to permit undue exposure or indecent movements in the dance are forbidden.

VII. DANCES

1. Dances suggesting or representing sexual actions or indecent passion are forbidden.
2. Dances which emphasize indecent movements are to be regarded as obscene.

VIII. RELIGION

1. No film or episode may throw **ridicule** on any religious faith.
2. **Ministers of religion** in their character as ministers of religion should not be used as comic characters or as villains.
3. **Ceremonies** of any definite religion should be carefully and respectfully handled.

IX. LOCATIONS

The treatment of bedrooms must be governed by good taste and delicacy.

X. NATIONAL FEELINGS

1. **The use of the flag** shall be consistently respectful.
2. **The history,** institutions, prominent people and citizenry of other nations shall be represented fairly.

XI. TITLES

Salacious, indecent, or obscene titles shall not be used.

XII. REPELLENT SUBJECTS

The following subjects must be treated within the careful limits of good taste:
1. **Actual hangings** or electrocutions as legal punishments for crime.
2. **Third Degree** methods.
3. **Brutality** and possible gruesomeness.
4. **Branding** of people or animals.
5. **Apparent cruelty** to children or animals.
6. **The sale of women,** or a woman selling her virtue.
7. **Surgical operations.**

REASONS SUPPORTING CODE

Reasons supporting a code to govern the making of motion and talking pictures formulated by Association of Motion Picture Producers, Inc., and The Motion Picture Producers and Distributors of America, Inc.

REASONS SUPPORTING PREAMBLE OF CODE

1. Theatrical motion pictures, that is, pictures intended for the theatre as distinct from pictures intended for churches, schools, lecture halls, educational movements, social reform movements, etc., are primarily to be regarded as entertainment.

Mankind has always recognized the importance of entertainment and its value in

rebuilding the bodies and souls of human beings.

But it has always recognized that entertainment can be of a character either helpful or harmful to the human race, and in consequence has clearly distinguished between:

a. Entertainment which tends to improve the race, or at least to re-create and rebuild human beings exhausted with the realities of life; and

b. Entertainment which tends to degrade human beings, or to lower their standards of life and living.

Hence the moral importance of entertainment is something which has been universal

Above: Joan Crawford epitomized the Jazz Age for all America in *Our Dancing Daughters* (1928).

Right: Advertised as 'The Most Daring Picture Ever Screened,' *Our Dancing Daughters*, in fact, only confirmed what the movies had helped to license throughout the decade – more freedom, more excitement, more power than women had ever had before.

exotic clothes and idealized relationships that bore no resemblance to everyday life.

The new Jazz Age films originated with Cecil B De Mille, who was the first to capitalize on the phenomena of short skirts, short hair, country clubs, night clubs, speakeasies, cocktail parties and the new morality. When World War I was ending, the Paramount head office had cabled him from New York to say: 'What the public demands today is modern stuff, with plenty of clothes, rich sets and action.' Paramount was right, and De Mille was the man to give the public what it wanted. He instructed his costume designers: 'I want clothes that will make people gasp when they see them. Don't design anything that anyone could buy in a store!' His films were the stuff of fantasy, combining a modern story with a flashback to ancient times – a technique that allowed for spectacle and depravity, but with the obligatory moral ending. Shipwrecked heiresses, Babylonian queens and slaves, rampaging lions and nude bathing sequences characterized the De Mille production, which became a byword for extravagance in the catch phrase 'a cast of thousands.' De Mille was a prime mover in the transition from the star system to the studio system.

War films were out of favor for several years, with such notable exceptions as Griffith's *Hearts of the World* (1918) and Chaplins's timeless *Shoulder Arms* (1918), both of which were released soon after the Armistice. After that, the subject was

after World War I, there was a shift away from the old rural, heroic and sentimental values that had prevailed in the early days. Exceptional movies like King Vidor's *The Crowd* (1928) gave a chilling picture of the vast depersonalization of big-city life, as experienced by a clerk working in a huge office where no one knows his name and everyone looks exactly alike. Ultimately, he loses his job and is swallowed up by the faceless masses of the city.

Edwardian novelist Elinor Glyn enjoyed enormous success in 1920s Hollywood because she was able to build a bridge between the old romanticism and the new morality. Sentimental dramas and comedies were affected by the new preoccupation with sex, personal freedom, material success and the emancipation of women (although the Wrong Girl continued to lose out to the self-effacing, hard-working and devoted heroine). But the main Hollywood product was aimed at the new, and newly prosperous, middle-class audience of the postwar years. Its cast of characters was a wholly imaginary leisured class in an elegant setting – beautiful homes, glamourous cars, fashionable and

Left: Cecil B De Mille directing *Fool's Paradise* – one of the lavish spectacles that he had pioneered – in 1922. Hollywood was hell-bent on fantasy, and consistency was no object. Balinese temple dancers, Babylonian hanging gardens and Indian elephants mingled happily in the same epics.

Below: Rudolph Valentino and Agnes Ayres in *The Sheik* (1921), the picture that set a new standard for masculine desirability. Valentino became a cult figure overnight, pursued by women, envied and emulated by men.

quiescent until King Vidor's *The Big Parade* (1925) proved that there was still an audience for the well-made war movie. For the most part, though, action was generated by the Western – America's nostalgic dream of its early innocence and the peace and freedom that had been sacrificed to urbanization and the automobile. Both the myth and the reality of the Old West were explored in hundreds of variations on the same theme: a good man pitted against a bad man who is terrorizing or corrupting the community, usually involving a rivalry between the two for the heroine, whom the hero wins by his moral and/or physical superiority over the man in the black hat and his various accomplices.

Costume dramas enjoyed a resurgence of popularity with vehicles like Fairbanks' *The Mark of Zorro* (1921) and Valentino's *The Sheik* (1921). The latent romanticism of the Jazz Age found an outlet in these dramas, and there was strong interest in stories of pimitive societies like Flaherty's *Nanook of the North* (1922) and the Fox production *Moana* (1923). The animated cartoon, which originated in 1909 with *Gertie the Dinosaur*, remained popular throughout the silent period. Felix the Cat and Koko the Clown were familiar favorites, and from 1925 onward, Walt Disney was producing such series as *Alice in Cartoonland* (1923-27), Oswald the Lucky Rabbit and Mortimer Mouse, soon to become Mickey Mouse, on the sound stage.

Both the technique and the content of Hollywood films became more sophisticated with the advent of European directors like Ernst Lubitsch, who came to America in 1922, and Erich von Stroheim, whose *Blind Husbands* (1919) and *Foolish Wives* (1922) struck a disturbing note of continental realism and cynicism about the marital relationship. The director's job became increasingly demanding as film technique evolved and the demands of Wall Street backers became more restrictive. Directing in the early days had been a casual affair. It was reported that Carl Laemmle instructed one of his producers about a forthcoming film to 'Let Jack Ford direct it. He yells good.' Most early directors were self-taught, and the successful ones met to some degree the standards defined by Thomas Ince, who said that 'The ideal director is one who, having pictured a scene in his mind, having tested it by putting himself into the various roles and getting reactions to those characters, still allows his cast enough scope to bring out additional touches that will add spontaneity to the interpretation and dramatic up-building ... Primarily the director must know life, but he must know, too, how to project life, not in narrative form, but by selected dramatic moments, each of which builds towards a definite crisis or climax that will bring a burst of emotional response from every audience.'

Ince was one of the first filmmakers to insist that his directors 'shoot the script as written,' rather than improvising as they went along in the manner of Griffith and Chaplin. As the movies became even bigger business, this budget- and control-consciousness increased.

In Hollywood's early days, almost everyone had been something else before he went into the risky business of making movies. Howard Hawks started out as an aviator, Raoul Walsh as a cowboy and Frank Capra as

Above: Erich von Stroheim (in costume) directs *Foolish Wives* (1922), in which he also starred as a lascivious member of the *ancien régime*. Stroheim's meticulous attention to detail made his films outstanding but expensive. He once spent three days teaching Hollywood extras how to salute in the style of the Austro-Hungarian Guards for a scene that would last only seconds.

Left: The magic of movie making revealed. King Vidor directs John Gilbert in *Bardleys the Magnificent* (1926).

Above: Independent producer David O Selznick began his career as an assistant to Jesse L Lasky, moved to Paramount, and then MGM, at which point he married Louis B Mayer's daughter, Irene. But it was sheer creativity, drive, and business acumen rather than nepotism that made him one of Hollywood's most successful image-makers.

a chemical engineer. Rouben Mamoulian was an exception: he had been a major New York and London theater director before he came to Hollywood to make *Applause* (1929). Despite his theater experience, which made him much sought after in the early days of sound, Mamoulian maintained that 'Film is primarily a graphic medium ... closer to painting than to the stage.'

F W Murnau was a leading German director when he made his first American film, *Sunrise*, for Fox in 1927. Another brilliant German director was Erich von Stroheim, who came to grief with the studio system. When he began working on his masterpiece, *Greed*, in 1924 for the Goldwyn Company, Samuel Goldwyn gave him a free hand in making the film faithful to the author's story. The result was 42 reels of film that would have run about eight hours. Von Stroheim cut the film down to 24 reels himself, then asked his friend Rex Ingram, director of the acclaimed *Four Horsemen of the Apocalypse* (1921), to cut it still further. Ingram returned 18 reels of film and a telegram that said, 'If you cut one more foot I shall never speak to you again.'

Meanwhile, the Goldwyn Company had become Metro-Goldwyn-Mayer, with Irving Thalberg as general manager, and the producer's authority had risen at the expense of the director's. As von Stroheim described the fate of *Greed*: 'I showed the telegram to Mr [Louis B] Mayer, who told me that he did not give a damn about Rex Ingram or me, and that the picture would be a total loss to the company anyway and must be cut to 10 reels ... It was given to a cutter, a man earning $30 a week, who had never read the book nor the script, and on whose mind was nothing but a hat. That man ruined my work of two years.'

This kind of experience was not unique to von Stroheim. As the studio system expanded, few directors exercised the kind of

Right: Charlie Chaplin (at camera) on location for *The Gold Rush* (1925), in which he played the Lone Prospector. Chaplin exercised complete creative control over his productions and was not only the most talented but the best-loved film personality of his day.

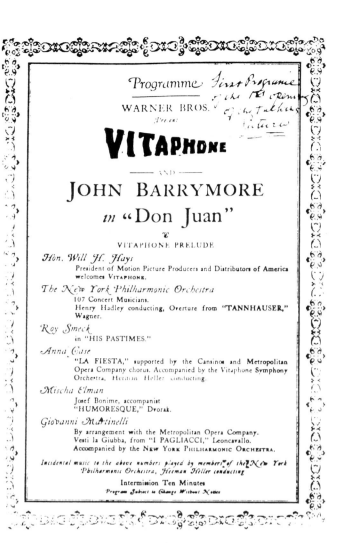

control enjoyed by the pioneers like Charlie Chaplin and Cecil B De Mille, who both directed and produced their films. Chaplin had begun his meteoric career with Sennett, but became an independent in 1919. He wrote, produced, directed and starred in his own films, which were so popular, both in the United States and abroad, that he could afford to spend a whole year on a single film. However, the experience of Pandro S Berman at MGM was more typical of the 1920s and '30s. He relates that 'Louis B Mayer used to say, "Give me a screenplay that I like and you've done your job as producer." He thought everything that was to be film footage should be on paper ... His filmmaking factory took over from there.'

Historically, the Hollywood producer has been caricatured as an overbearing, cigar-chomping vulgarian shouting into three telephones at once beside a pool in Beverly Hills. Producers got a bad press in novels like F Scott Fitzgerald's *The Last Tycoon* and Budd Schulberg's *What Makes Sammy Run?* One reason that it was so easy to portray the producer as a mercenary hustler was that his function was not clearly understood by the general public. David O Selznick, once of the most successful producers in Hollywood

history, emphasized the role of the producer as creator rather than businessman. He held that 'The producer ... must be able, if necessary, to sit down and write the scene, and if he is criticizing a director he must be able not merely to say 'I don't like it,' but tell him how he would direct it himself. He must be able to go into a cutting room, and if he doesn't like the cutting of the sequence ... he must be able to recut.' But Selznick was an independent, and by the 1930s, perhaps only he and Samuel Goldwyn among the major image makers, had the technical expertise and creativity to supervise every detail of every film they produced. For the most part, the director/producer roles became increasingly distinct, and many directors suffered the fate described by George Stevens, who observed that 'When the movie industry was young, the filmmaker was its core and the man who handled the business details his partner ... When he finally looked around, he found his partner's name on the door. Thus the film-maker became the employee, and the man who had time to attend to the details became the head of the studio.'

Meanwhile, the sound revolution was effecting a complete transition in the history of the movies. When sound films had become

Above: The program for Warner Bros.' Vitaphone production of *Don Juan*, presented with great fanfare at the Manhattan Opera House in New York in 1926. The novelty of recorded musical accompaniment to a silent film was Harry Warner's main selling point to exhibitors, who remained reluctant to invest in the expensive Vitaphone equipment for their theaters – until *The Jazz Singer* was released the following year.

technically feasible, in the early 1920s, Hollywood had resisted the disruption and expense of changing its production and distribution methods. Then the Warner brothers, who were struggling to make their studio a major force on a shoestring budget, gambled on sound as a means of reproducing music without the expense of live performers. In 1926 they released *Don Juan* and several shorts with musical accompaniment on discs synchronized with each reel. Taking their cue, Fox introduced sound-on-film newsreels. But silent films were already accompanied by live music and sound effects. The missing link was dialogue, as shown by the growing popularity of radio. When Al Jolson improvised the line 'You ain't heard nothing yet' in *The Jazz Singer* (1927), the silent movie was destined for history as an art form.

The Jazz Singer was an enormous success, and Warner's daring gamble on the Vitaphone process paid off in a matter of months at the box office. By the summer of 1928, 300 theaters were wired to show the first 'talkies' and other studios rushed to secure equipment, build soundproof stages and force their silent stars to speak, with varying degrees of success. Some careers were ended, others took off like a comet.

As David Robinson has observed, 'The cinema of the years between 1918 and 1928 presents a record which would be astonishing in any art form.' Richard Griffith expressed well the sense of loss that came with the end of the silent period: 'Whatever improvements it

might have developed if it had survived a few years longer, the silent film at its best had by 1928 attained singular completeness as a human experience. To walk into a darkened theatre, to focus upon a bright rectangle of moving light, to listen somewhat below the level of consciousness to music which was no longer good or bad in itself, but merely in relation to what was on the screen, and above all to watch, in a kind of charmed, hypnotic trance, a pattern of images which appeared and disappeared as capriciously as those pictures which involuntarily present them-

Above: The men who made the sound revolution, left and right, Harry M and Samuel L Warner, flanked by Will Hays and Walter C Rich, president of the Vitaphone Corporation. The occasion was the 1926 world premiere of the Vitaphone process, during which Hays predicted timidly that sound would usher in a new era of 'pictures and music.'

Far left: Clark Gable and Mary Astor watch with approval as co-star Jean Harlow films a close-up on the set of *Red Dust* (1932). Gable and Harlow made a series of popular romantic comedies together and were filming *Saratoga* when Harlow died in 1937.

Left: MGM's famous Leo the Lion emits his first roar as the studio's trademark, faithfully recorded by an apprehensive-looking team of technicians.

Above: Three of the four incomparable Marx brothers, identified in their typically wacky style. Missing from the picture is Zeppo, the straight man. The word 'script' had no meaning in a Marx Brothers vehicle. Scene after scene was improvised to hilarious effect, as hapless co-stars struggled to keep up – or even upright.

Far right: The beautiful Jeanette MacDonald being directed by Rouben Mamoulian in *Love Me Tonight* (1932). Cameraman Victor Milner, bottom right, observes. Mamoulian's theater experience made him much sought after when sound came in.

selves to the mind as it is droppng off to sleep … this was an experience complete and unique, radically unlike that provided by the older arts or by the other new media of mass communication. It bade fair to become the characteristic art-experience of our time.'

However, the sensitivity of these critics to what was lost with the passing of the silent film was not generally shared by the public, which responded enthusiastically to the advent of sound. Warners followed up the success of *The Jazz Singer* almost immediately with *The Singing Fool* (1928), which had substantial talking sequences. The all-talking picture came in with their *Lights of New York* (1928), in which the dialogue was non-stop, and the Warners put three million dollars into a trust fund for themselves and led a reluctant industry into talking pictures.

Despite the fact that the clumsy new sound equipment had a disastrous effect upon the artistic quality of Hollywood films in the first few years, the image makers rushed to market with dialogue films and musicals. Broadway was raided for actors who could speak, and plays were transferred bodily to the cinema with little regard for their suitability to the medium. Many of the imported actors proved unsuited to the more intimate medium of film, although some enjoyed a success that led to a whole new generation of Hollywood stars, including Edward G Robinson, Fredric March, Paul Muni and James Cagney. Silent-film idols like Douglas Fairbanks Sr and Mary Pickford found their careers losing momentum, while other artists – Norma Shearer, Ronald Colman and Janet Gaynor, to name a few – were on the ascendant.

Undeniably, some of the studios used sound films as an excuse to get rid of actors whom they no longer wanted to keep under contract, on the ground that their voices or personalities were unsuited to sound. John Gilbert is frequently cited as an example of this, since his successful career foundered in the early 1930s despite his more than adequate performances in talking pictures. (But the whole story of Gilbert's decline and fall would not be told until his daughter, Leatrice Joy Gilbert, published her biography *Dark Star*.)

Some of the silent-screen giants proceeded cautiously into the new medium. Chaplin's *City Lights* (1931) and *Modern Times* (1936) were really silent films with some degree of synchronised musical and sound effects. Not until 1941 did Chaplin make a full-scale talking picture – *The Great Dictator*. Staple genres like slapstick comedy were on the wane, and new styles evolved. Laurel and Hardy made a successful transition to talking pictures, and the Marx Brothers invented a whole comic language. Beginning with *Broadway Melody* (1929), a new kind of film that owed its very existence to sound came into being, the Hollywood musical. And gangster films leaped into prominence with the addition of colorful speech idioms to the pictorial representation of the exciting Jazz Age underworld.

Within a few years, the deficiencies of the new medium were being resolved by Hollywood artists. The inventive Rouben Mamoulian put the camera on wheels to restore the mobility lost when it had to be enclosed in great soundproof booths. Better microphone systems released actors from their anchorage within range of hidden mikes, obviating the static quality that characterized the early talking pictures. In *Hallelujah!* (1929), King Vidor demonstrated that dialogue and song could be used for dramatic effects no less powerful than those he had achieved with images alone in *The Big Parade* and *The Crowd*. Ernst Lubitsch found vast potential in the new medium, and proved it by remaking his *Marriage Circle* as *One Hour With You* (1932). And some of the silent-screen idols – Greta Garbo is perhaps the best example – moved serenely into the age of sound with no diminution of their triumphant artistry.

The novelty of sound brought movie attendance to record levels and staved off the competition presented by radio. Films became the nation's fourth largest industry. Although theater attendance slumped in the dark early days of the Depression, cheaper tickets, double bills and 'dish-night' give-aways helped ensure an early recovery. All but the most indigent could afford the price of a brief escape from reality, and most availed themselves of the opportunity. As Arthur

Above: Marlene Dietrich and Charles Boyer on location in Yuma, Arizona, for Selznick's *The Garden of Allah* (1936).

Below: A detail of the striking set for *Top Hat* (1935), typical of those designed for RKO musicals starring Fred Astaire and Ginger Rogers.

Schlesinger Jr wrote about this period 'When the Movies Really Counted': 'Hollywood possessed the nation. It formed our images and shaped our dreams ... The announcement of new movies created anticipation and suspense. The art was bursting with ideas and vitality and point. Young men sauntered down the street like James Cagney, wise-cracked like William Powell, cursed like Humphrey Bogart and wooed like Clark Gable; young women laughed like Lombard and sighed like Garbo, and looked (or tried to look) like Hedy Lamarr.'

During the early 1930s, gangster movies filled the screen with violence and sex, and exotic locales transported Depression-weary audiences into another realm for a magical hour or two. When Franklin Delano Roosevelt's New Deal rallied the nation's hope of recovery in 1933, Hollywood shifted its emphasis from gangsters to G-men and from the exotic to the wholesome. This change went hand in hand with the tough new production code enforced as a result of the formation of the Roman Catholic Legion of Decency.

The Depression years also brought a vast migration of musical talent from Broadway to Hollywood, including George and Ira Gershwin and Cole Porter. The old theater prejudice against 'the flickers' had been done away by improved film technology, high salaries and participation in the exciting new medium by a host of talented professionals. The extravagant song-and-dance spectacles staged by Busby Berkeley, and the sparkling Fred Astaire and Ginger Rogers musicals produced by RKO epitomized glamour and fantasy for the movie-going public. Berkeley used the screen as a canvas, on which he painted intricate patterns of movement to complement the new possibilities of movie music.

Art direction had become important when the Glamour Years began, and the acknowledged master was Cedric Gibbons, who had begun his work with Edison in 1914, joined Goldwyn in 1918 and moved to MGM in 1924. As supervising art director, he headed an art department that included up to 200 art directors and draftsmen, scene and matte painters. He was responsible for the stylistic consistency that made MGM pictures stand out and was a major force in the popularization of art deco as a symbol of taste and style. White-on-white decor, as introduced by decorator Syrie Maugham, and large opulent sets characterized the MGM movies from the mid-1920s into the 1930s.

At Paramount, art director Hans Drier, who had started with UFA Studios in Germany, teamed with brilliant foreign-born directors like Ernst Lubitsch and Joseph von Sternberg to produce an atmosphere of elegance and Continental sophistication. As Lubitsch himself remarked: 'There is Paramount Paris and Metro Paris, and of course the real Paris. Paramount's is the most Parisian of all.'

Trend-setting designers like Lyle Wheeler started national fads with streamlined sets

that reflected the 1930s love affair with *art moderne*. Wheeler's sleek nightclub set for Selznick's *The Young in Heart* (1937) made instant fashion accessories of blond wood, chrome and glass brick, which dominated Hollywood nightclubs and houses.

Above: Art director Cedric Gibbons with one of the many awards his taste and style garnered for MGM during the 1920s and 1930s.

Left: Production designer William Cameron Menzies (left) and Lyle Wheeler, art director for Selznick International Pictures, review the 1500 watercolor sketches prepared for *Gone With The Wind* (1939).

38

Above: Top Hat (1935): a panoramic view of the 'Big White Set' for the streets of Venice designed to showcase the dancing of Astaire and Rogers.

Right: Jean Harlow, in the tight satin sheath that became her trademark, relaxes on a reclining board as she confers with George Cukor on the set of *Dinner at Eight* (1933). Every second woman in America would want a dress just as glamorous and uncomfortable.

The tight budget at Warner Bros., and stories 'ripped from the headlines,' were a challenge to art director Anton Grot, an immigrant from Poland. Influenced by German Expressionism, he framed his actors against vast expanses of wall and ceiling, and made menacing use of shadow and forced perspective. Many Hollywood sets from the period were used again and again – some are still in use, like Universal's set for *The Phantom of the Opera* (1925) and New York streets on the lot at Twentieth Century Fox. Nathanael West gave a haunting description of the eerie atmosphere of the back lot in his classic novel of Hollywood, *The Day of the Locust*: 'He pushed his way through a tangle of briars, old flats, and iron junk, skirting the skeleton of a zeppelin, a bamboo stockade, an adobe fort, the wooden horse of Troy, a flight of baroque palace stairs that started in a bed of weeds and ended against the branches of an oak, part of the Fourteenth Street elevated station, a Dutch windmill, the bones of a dinosaur, the upper half of the *Merrimac*, a corner of a Mayan temple, until he finally reached the road.'

RKO pictures were renowned for their inventiveness, including the striking black-and-white sets that showed off the dancing of Astaire and Rogers to such advantage. Creative sets like those for *King Kong* (1932) and *Citizen Kane* (1941) were tours de force in special effects and production design. To save money, many of the splendors of *Citizen Kane*'s mansion, Xanadu, were produced by optical illusion.

Hollywood started innumerable fashion trends during the Glamour Years, when stars like Jean Harlow wore skin-tight satin sheaths that made it impossible for them to sit down. They had to relax on reclining boards with slanted footrests between takes. But American women took the uncomfortable style to their hearts, and bias-cut satin sheaths were seen at the most fashionable parties in the country. When Joan Crawford appeared in a ruffled-shoulder dress designed by Adrian for *Letty Lynton* (1932), Macy's sold 50,000 copies. And Crawford's favored padded-shoulder look dominated the decade's fashions. As *Vogue* magazine told its readers in 1937: 'The way you make up your

Above: The impressive line-up of Paramount stars of 1931, prepared by studio publicists to keep their personalities in the public eye. The competition for media attention was relentless.

Right: Matinee idol Wallace Reid and svelte Gloria Swanson pose with the elegant British novelist Elinor Glyn, who made 'It' a synonym for sex appeal in her screenplays. Glyn was one of the few writers from another medium to achieve major success in Hollywood.

lips, apply your rouge ... ten to one it came from Hollywood and was designed for some famous star.' *Silver Screen* enthused, 'Have you the secret wish to become a beautiful island enchantress? Well, lovely Dorothy Lamour's slinky native sarongs will soon be available to every plain Jane.' Carole Lombard popularized lounging pajamas, and Marlene Dietrich created a passion for slacks. Screen goddess Lana Turner gave the sweater a new lease on life.

The 1930s saw the rapid rise of Irving Thalberg, MGM's *wunderkind* producer, who presided over the studio that described itself as having 'more stars than there are in heaven.' They included Greta Garbo, Clark Gable, William Powell, Norma Shearer (Thalberg's wife), Crawford, Harlow, Lionel and John Barrymore, Charles Laughton, the Marx Brothers, W C Fields, Wallace Beery, Spencer Tracy, Lamarr, Myrna Loy, and such 'Hollywood kids' as Elizabeth Taylor, Mickey Rooney, Judy Garland and Ava Gardner. At Paramount, Gary Cooper, Charles Boyer, Claudette Colbert and Dietrich were featured players, while Warner Bros. had James Cagney, Pat O'Brien, Edward G Robinson and Bette Davis under contract.

Nepotism remained a fact of life at most of the Hollywood studios, as it had been since the industry began. Anita Loos tells the story of how Columbia Pictures imported playwright Augustus Thomas, author of *The Witching Hour*, to doctor some shaky scripts that had defied the talents of studio sons and daughters, cousins and in-laws. Harry Cohn, head of the studio, handed a pile of these scripts to Thomas when he arrived from New York with instructions to set them right. Thomas returned from a weekend's work with every comma in place, and Cohn was aghast. He stormed into his office yelling, 'Augustus Thomas has straightened out six plots in only three days. Get the s.o.b. on the first train to New York before he wrecks my family life!'

The 1930s saw a continuation of Hollywood's traditional love/hate relationship with its screenwriters. Many of the most successful writers of the silent era had been women, including Metro's June Mathis, who wrote some of the best Valentino screenplays; Frances Marion, a close friend of Mary Pickford's, who adapted *The Scarlet Letter* (1926) and the immortal *The Wind* (1928) and Lenore Coffee, who became even better known as a writer of talking pictures. Anita Loos was writing up story ideas for Biograph at the age of 15, and her brilliant career spans most of Hollywood history. Loos subtitled D W Griffith's epic 'message movie' *Intolerance* (1916), whose spectacular Babylonian

sets loomed over East Hollywood for years after the picture was released. She recalled later that 'I must be honest and say I thought D W had lost his mind ... The story of *Intolerance* jumped back and forth between four different periods of time with nothing to tie the pieces together except its theme of man's inhumanity to man.' Audiences shared her bewilderment and the project was set down as an impressive failure.

In the early 1920s, Hollywood had invited distinguished writers like Maurice Maeterlinck, Rex Beach, Elinor Glyn and Michael Arlen to lend their talents to the film industry. But with the exception of Edwardian novelist Glyn, who invented 'It' as a synonym for sex appeal in the person of Clara Bow, writers from other media achieved little except as window dressing.

By the mid-1920s, the lure of big money was attracting members of New York's Algonquin Round Table and talented journalists from the New York and Chicago papers. Herman Mankiewicz came out from the *Chicago Tribune* and found that he had detrained where the streets were paved with gold. He cabled his friend and colleague Ben

Below: Screenwriter Anita Loos, left, was writing for Biograph in her teens and became a celebrity with *Gentlemen Prefer Blondes*, produced for both stage and screen. New York man-about-town Wilson Mizner appeared in the Paramount screen version with Ruth Taylor, who had the role of Lorelei Lee.

Left: Screenwriter Ben Hecht, right, confers with Fredric March, left, and Walter Connolly on the storyline of *Nothing Sacred* (1937), a brilliant satire on publicity stunts that co-starred Carole Lombard. Hecht's experience in journalism made him well suited to the high-pressure profession of screenwriting.

Hecht: 'Will you accept three hundred per week to work for Paramount Pictures? All expenses paid. The three hundred is peanuts. Millions are to be grabbed out here and your only competition is idiots. Don't let this get around.' Hecht promptly complied, and made a fortune writing major screenplays that included *Scarface* (1932) and *The Front Page* (1931). He also worked without credit on *Gone With The Wind* (1939), written at top speed after the original script was discarded by producer David O Selznick, and his million-dollar cast was immobilized to the tune of $50,000 a day. As Hecht described the experience: 'Twenty-four-hour work shifts were quite common under David's baton. David himself sometimes failed to go to bed for several nights in a row. He preferred to wait until he collapsed on his office couch. Medication was often necessary to revive him.' Ultimately, 14 screenwriters, including F Scott Fitzgerald, collaborated on the epic Civil War film.

Some of America's best-known writers 'did time' in Hollywood during the 1920s and '30s, including the irrepressible Dorothy Parker, who had made her reputation as a humorist at Frank Crowninshield's *Vanity Fair* and Harold Ross's *New Yorker*. (Parker reportedly leaned out the window of her studio's writers' building and screamed 'Let me out! I'm as sane as you are!') William Faulkner, who requested permission to work at home when he came to Hollywood, was

Left: Independent producer Samuel Goldwyn was the despair of his writers. His enthusiasm for a storyline could turn into aversion overnight, and he was constantly firing and rehiring his frazzled staff. Signing a Goldwyn contract is Miriam Hopkins, observed by Eddie Cantor, the star of *Kid Millions* (1935).

Right: Humorist Dorothy Parker, with her husband, Alan Campbell, a writer and actor, arrive from New York to prepare the screenplay for *Lady Beware*, a Bing Crosby vehicle for Paramount.

44

Above: Director Frank Capra, left, on the set of *Mr Deeds Goes to Town* (1936) with a rangy young Gary Cooper. Capra began his career directing Westerns and believed that they were the basic movie form from which all else had followed.

the object of a frantic manhunt at his studio – until someone remembered that he lived in Oxford, Mississippi. Nathanael West drew on his screenwriting experience for his memorable *Day of the Locust*, and John Steinbeck, Robert Sherwood, Robert Benchley and Clifford Odets all had their day in the land of make-believe. However, most screenwriters were not famous; they were merely hardworking, capable and adaptable. Story conferences throughout the scripting process could ring in changes proposed – or demanded – by the producer, director, star, or studio head. Twenty-hour days were not uncommon when a picture got into trouble during shooting, and writers at Paramount had to deliver 11 pages a week if they wanted to keep their jobs. Often, the final version was unrecognizable. As William Holden, playing a screenwriter in *Sunset Boulevard* (1950), remarked: 'The last one I wrote was about Oakies in the Dust Bowl. You'd never know, because when it reached the screen, the whole thing played on a torpedo boat.'

In *Kiss Hollywood Goodbye*, Anita Loos recalled the hazards of working with the volatile Sam Goldwyn, whose enthusiasms could be even more alarming than his rejections. 'When I brought Sam a first outline, he beamed. "Dot's beautifool. I adore your story line. Go ahead and write me a sample scene." But a few days later, when I read the scene to Sam, he exploded, "Dat story line stinks! Vot are you trying to do to me? Ruin Gary Cooper?" It was a regular occurrence to be fired by Sam, but he always followed it with a fawning reinstatement ... Then, too, there was always the comic relief of Sam's classic bloopers, such as his boast: "I vant you to know that a Goldvyn comedy is not to be laughed at!"'

David Niven, too, found the great independent producer unnerving when he came to Hollywood in the mid-1930s and attracted Goldwyn's attention. As Niven recalled, 'He was almost entirely bald, very well dressed, with small intense eyes set in a brown face ... He spoke without smiling in a strangley high-pitched voice.' The two had numerous fights and reconciliations from the day that Louella Parsons announced 'GOLDWYN SIGNS UNKNOWN!' But the engaging British actor did not remain unknown for long, and he left a unique chronicle of Glamour Years Hollywood in his books *The Moon's a Balloon* and *Bring on the Empty Horses*.

Of his early years in the film capital, Niven reported that 'John McClain was at the Garden of Allah, so I rented a bungalow there, and although I missed F Scott Fitzgerald, who had moved to Malibu with Sheilah Graham, I had the great joy of meeting Robert Benchley and Dorothy Parker ... There had been a big influx of 'Easterners,' and I spent fascinating evenings at Cole Porter's house, where it was quite usual to listen to Cole or Irving Berlin or George Gershwin playing numbers from the half-written scores of their future smash hit musicals.'

Niven also joined the Hollywood Cricket Club and played polo with Darryl F Zanuck, who became the first head of Twentieth Century-Fox in 1935. *Fortune* magazine followed the high-powered producer through a typical day for its readers. 'Wherever Zanuck goes, there are dictaphones: in his bedroom, in his office, in the projection rooms where he sees what he has wrought. His genius is one of self-expression.' Zanuck was a product of the studio system, and he exercised tight control over both the creative and financial sides of his films. Neither his producers nor his writers challenged his authority within the studio. In the end, though, Zanuck used his position as a springboard into the coveted role of independent producer, backed by financial and distribution guarantees from a studio.

Left: Polo buffs, from left, Spencer Tracy, Walt Disney, Darryl Zanuck and Frank Borzage line up for a day's sport in the mid-1930s. Polo was a popular pastime with Hollywood's affluent outdoor set.

Below: Portly British director Alfred Hitchcock ponders the staging of a scene for *Rebecca*, his first American film, with Joan Fontaine, seated at table. The successful 1940 film launched Hitchcock's American career, which lasted for the rest of his life.

Richard Zanuck, his son, followed the same path. Frank Capra remained a successful director into the Depression days when his films, including *Mr Deeds Goes to Town* (1936), made a hero of the ordinary man – in this case Gary Cooper. In 1940 Alfred Hitchcock came to the United States as an established director of outstanding British suspense films. His first American film was *Rebecca* (1940), for David O Selznick, which launched a 40-year career in US movies and television. Hitchcock's pear-shaped profile and lugubrious speech were fixtures of American entertainment, and he made frequent cameo appearances in his movies.

As David Niven described his share in the Glamour Years, 'There was an excitement and generosity of spirit in Hollywood – a minimum of jealousy and pettiness; everyone felt they were still pioneering in a wonderful entertainment medium. The premieres of the big pictures were black-tie events, and all the big names turned out to cheer on their friends. Outside, bleachers were erected to enable the screaming fans to catch a glimpse of their favorites, and searchlights wove patterns across the sky.' By the end of the 1930s, the giant studios were featuring their star players in up to 10 films a year. Quantity, variety and excellence had made Hollywood movies known around the world. For the image makers, as David McClintock points out, 'the driving forces were elemental – power, money, fame ... and an opportunity to have a great deal of fun in the pursuit of these pleasures.'

When Prohibition finally became law on 30 June 1919, Hollywood staged its own gala farewell to legal drinking. Tables that normally went for two dollars apiece at the Vernon Country Club had a fifty-dollar price tag on that fatal Sunday night. All roads into the resort town of Venice were blocked by some 100,000 determined revelers, and tables at the popular Ship Cafe went for $300 apiece. Impromptu parades snaked through the streets. When the taps were turned off at midnight, an explosion of fireworks, auto horns and whistles signaled the fact that California was 'dry.' But the whole celebration turned out to be a beginning rather than an end. It ushered in a new era of rumrunning, speakeasies, gambling and general abandon that saw all America in a state of adolescent rebellion.

In Vernon, Jack Doyle's closed but the Vernon Country Club boomed right along, advising patrons to 'bring your own.' The Ship sailed merrily through the 1920s in defiance of the law. Cabarets, speakeasies and nightclubs mushroomed in Culver City, which was becoming a second Hollywood as additional studios established themselves there. During the 1920s, MGM, Willat, Triangle Studios and Hal Roach settled in and around Washington Boulevard, which was one of the main arteries between Los Angeles and the beach towns. Nearby Venice Boulevard was serviced by the Pacific Electric's Red Car tracks, so Culver City was accessible to all of what was called the Southland, and movie folk abounded there. Its autonomy made it attractive to entrepreneurs who were profiting from the legal moratorium on night life.

Official 'dining spots' like Ford's Castle and Moonlite Gardens featured covert gin and extroverted jazz. The open-air ballroom called Danceland featured Speed Webb and his Colored Melody Lads. There was so much space around it that Danceland advertised parking for 3000 cars, for much of the region was still farmland. In 1923 contractor Dan Coombs began work on the Green Mill at Washington and National Boulevards. A pseudo-Norman castle, the Mill would become popular with the film colony; in 1926 it became Frank Sebastian's Cotton Club, the biggest nightspot in Prohibition-era Los Angeles. By that date, Culver City's rural Broadway had attracted any number of bootleggers, prostitutes, gamblers and other dubious characters into the area. Uninhibited nightlife flourished at the DooDoo Inn, the Kit Kat Club, Monkey Farm, the Hoosegow, Harlow's Cafe, the Midnight Frolics and the Sneak Inn. These were supplied liberally by the rumrunners who plied the coast. The town of Playa del Rey was a popular landing place for the illegal supplies that kept the party going.

Restauranteur Frank Sebastian had opened a successful cafe on Windward Avenue in Venice, and when he took over the Green Mill and made it a showcase for black jazz bands and 'Creole Revues,' Hollywood flocked to hear and see them. Advertised as 'The King of Cabarets,' Sebastian's Cotton Club was to the film colony what Harlem was to New York. Entertainers like Les Hite, Lionel Hampton, Cab Calloway, Duke Ellington and Louis Armstrong made the new club part of their tours, along with New York, Chicago and New Orleans. Up to 2000 patrons could be accommodated in the lavishly appointed club, which Sebastian redecorated in an eclectic style ranging from Omar Khayam to French chateau (the exterior was outlined in neon). New Year's Eve there was an extra-special event, with three dance bands on separate floors, four big-name revues, souvenirs and favors and a sumptuous breakfast for those who survived the all-night festivities, which cost between $5.00 and $7.50 per person. It was also rumored that gambling was available in the back room, and slot machines were openly displayed in the lobby for a time. 'Bad publicity' like Louis

Previous pages: Serial star Ruth Roland (center, in checked cap), throws a costume party at the Plantation Club in Culver City (1929).

Below: Vibrant, red-haired Clara Bow was an enthusiastic member of the film colony's baseball team in 1926.

Armstrong's arrest for possession of marijuana only increased the club's business. (Armstrong was set free to play another day.)

The Planatation Cafe, financed by Fatty Arbuckle after his success with the Mack Sennett comedy troupe, lived up to its name with an imposing pillared facade in the best Hollywood Southern tradition. An attractively planted fountain ornamented the spacious circular drive, and the antebellum mansion played host to some of Hollywood's most popular stars in the not-so-silent era.

The Ambassador Hotel provided deluxe lodging in 400 rooms and bungalows and played host during the 1920s to Wilson Mizner, John Barrymore, Pola Negri, Norma Talmadge and many others who visited Hollywood or settled there. The Zinnia Grill, on the hotel's Casino level, was a popular gathering place for film celebrities and other guests who wanted a glimpse of them. In the growing trend toward exoticism, the grill's walls were covered with black satin handpainted with colorful zinnias and the club was called the "Black Patent Leather Room". The adjoining Parrot Porch featured live tropical birds and plants.

The Ambassador management correctly divined that the hotel could support a full-scale nightclub, and plans were made to convert the Grand Ballroom into the Cocoanut Grove. There was seating for a thousand patrons, and the club's decor was kept a secret till opening night – 21 April 1921.

Above: Cab Calloway and his popular orchestra made the long trek from Harlem to appear at Frank Sebastian's Cotton Club at Washington and National Boulevards.

Left: Roscoe Arbuckle's stylish Plantation Club remained a major Hollywood nightspot long after its owner fell from grace in the industry.

Above: The unmistakable facade of Musso and Frank's Grill was a Prohibition-era landmark.

Below: The Ambassador Hotel's Cocoanut Grove was an immediate hit when it opened in 1921; it became a byword for exciting night life.

First-nighters found themselves in a Pacific paradise, complete with life-size imitation palm trees nailed to the hardwood floor. Strings of colored lanterns, imitation monkeys scrambling among the trees and a mural of tropical mountains and waterfalls heightened the effect. (Later, a *Photoplay* article would reveal that the Cocoanut Grove's palm trees were left over from the filming of Rudolph Valentino's *The Sheik*.)

The whole concept was an immediate hit, especially since the hotel had a liberal, if unofficial, liquor policy. Suitcases laden with illegal supplies materialized from a long line of limousines at the hotel's porte cochere on the night of a big party, and guests who had planned ahead would be reunited with their refreshments by reaching under the table. Movie stars had their choice of providing impromptu entertainment or of making the grandest possible entrance, especially on Tuesday nights, when elaborate floor shows accompanied the mass influx of the film colony.

The Cocoanut Grove's Charleston contests were a staple of 1920s night life. Joan Crawford and her partner, Michael Cudahy, whose family had made a fortune in meat-packing, competed hotly against Jean Peters (before she became Carole Lombard) and her partner. Both were just getting started in the movies, and the Grove was the ideal place to be seen. Other contestants were more interested in the silver trophies that were awarded: May McAvoy parlayed hers into $300 worth of cash.

The Grove had opened with Art Hickman's jazz band, and it continued the tradition with Abe Lyman, Ted Fio Rito, Gus Arnheim and other popular white jazz musicians. The first floor show was presented

almost a year after the club opened: it featured Maurice and Lenora Hughes with their acclaimed Continental skating waltz. They were soon followed by a well-known mental telepathist (this was in the age of Coué, who made a cult of the power of positive thinking), then by a 'Great Night Frolic' in the tradition of Florenz Ziegfeld's revues. Friday night was Collegiate Night, with more dance contests and a pitcher of tropical punch that was easily spiked from a hip flask.

The Ambassador spared no effort to increase the attractions of the Cocoanut Grove, the first real 'Playground of the Stars.' Floor shows featured scantily clad chorines who circled the dance floor on elaborate floats. Expensive dolls were positioned in centerpieces as favors, and toy monkeys descended from the balcony on strings to set off wild scrambles for prizes among the rich and famous. The Grove got a reputation early on for brawling, which only enhanced its appeal in an age that flouted all the conventions. The Ambassador's location in the heart of downtown Los Angeles made it more accessible than the isolated roadhouses and beach resorts – one was sure of a large audience there.

In 1922 W E Kreiter opened the Cinderella Rooftop Ballroom on Sixth Street in Los Angeles. Farther out, the Venice Ballroom remained a popular rendezvous, especially for those in search of privacy. Hollywood itself now had much more to offer than it had in the film colony's early days. Increasing numbers of tourists congregated there to gawk at the stars, whom they hoped to find in every side street and watering hole. The new money generated by the movie industry was a magnet for entertainment ventures.

Musso and Frank's had been a gathering place for the stars for some years when Eddie Brandstatter, of Sunset Inn fame, opened the Montmartre Cafe on the second floor of 6757 Hollywood Boulevard. It quickly became a favored spot for long, elaborate lunches, especially on Wednesdays, when Brandstatter catered to the film trade. Fans crowded the spacious cafe's entrance, hoping for a glimpse of their favorite stars, who came to enjoy the Montmartre's elegant ambience and good food. Three hundred and fifty patrons could be seated in the spacious dining room, which was decorated with crystal chandeliers and carpets imported from Europe; the combined solid-silver service weighed over a ton. The Montmartre also offered hot jazz and the obligatory Charleston contests in the evenings. Joan Crawford shimmied here when not at the Cocoanut Grove, and Valentino dined with Winifred Hudnut and her dog. Visiting dignitaries signed the guest book as well: Winston Churchill, the King of Sweden and Prince George of England.

Coffee Dan's was a basement Latin Quarter-type cabaret that was entered by sliding down a chute. Popular apache dancers wound their sinuous way among fake boulder pillars, and the murky light concealed a lot of stars who loved the bogus bohemian atmosphere. Ham and eggs were the staple of the menu, accompanied by lively jazz bands. A comparable evening was provided by the Paris Inn, Hollywood's answer to the Left Bank, which opened late in 1924 'in the shadow of City Hall,' in downtown Los Angeles. Singing waiters addressed arias to both the 'Renaissance' and 'Bohemian' sides of the cafe, and sketch artists complete with smocks and berets made caricatures of famous patrons. The Eiffel Tower dominated an atmospheric mural of a Parisian street scene.

Out of town, the San Fernando Valley scorned fake palm trees and fancy clothes,

Above: The elegant Montmartre Cafe spared no expense on decor and service. It quickly became a popular gathering place for long lunches and evenings of jazz.

Below: Crowds gather on Hollywood Boulevard in the hope of seeing celebrities arrive for lunch at the Montmartre.

offering instead the Zulu Hut – a thatched-roof compound presided over by 'Zulu Chief' Raymond McKee and his staff of waiters in black-face. Apparent confusion between darkest Africa and the Deep South resulted in a menu consisting mainly of fried chicken and cornpone, but patrons made it a popular haunt in cheerful disregard of any inconsistency. Drive-ups became popular along southern California's highways, since dining in the privacy of one's own roadster solved any problem with liquor service – self-serve was the rule. Establishments like Pumpkin's, the Chili Bowl and the Lighthouse dispensed sandwiches and snacks. An elaborate chiliburger could be had at Ptomaine Tommy's, on Broadway, where the sporting crowd congregated after polo or prize fights. The White Spot, at Wilshire and La Brea, was another glorified hamburger stand favored by the film crowd. But some malcontents, including Jack Warner, complained that Hollywood night life was still not up to snuff. Warner told Herbert Somborn and Wilson Mizner that there was 'no really first-class restaurant where actors of lofty eminence could dine in relative privacy,' and the three set out to remedy this lack.

Somborn purchased the property opposite the Ambassador Hotel, Warner came up with financial backing and Mizner supplied the atmosphere (that of New York's Jack Dunstan's before the descent of Prohibition). There are several stories about how the new

Above: Both film stars and Los Angeles society women made it a point to be seen at the Montmartre for the fashionable Wednesday luncheon.

Right: Hollywood couldn't seem to stop dressing up in costumes, even on its own time. This gala was hosted by the Darryl F Zanucks in the late 1920s.

restaurant got its name, the best known of which is Somborn's observation that 'You could open a restaurant in an alley and call it anything, if the food and service were good, the patrons would just come flocking. It would even be called something as ridiculous as the Brown Derby.' In fact, the new restaurant was constructed to look exactly like the popular hat and was named accordingly. Hollywood took it to its collective heart immediately.

The original Brown Derby seated a hundred people in its surprisingly modest interior. Booths lined the walls, and in the center was a counter that encircled a service area. The cashier was stationed near the door and offered gum, cigars and tickets for 'theatres, fites and amusements.' Light fixtures in the shape of derby hats hung over each booth, and the witty Wilson Mizner presided over his counterpart of the Algonquin Round Table in Booth 50, where he held forth almost daily for seven years. A sometime writer at several studios, Mizner's chief stock in trade was repartee, storytelling and verbal assaults on every Derby customer. Regulars at his court included George Jessel, Mae Murray, Charlie Chaplin, W C Fields and Darryl Zanuck. The Brown Derby soon edged out other dining spots and increased its ascendancy by staying open until four o'clock in the morning, thus attracting everyone who had survived the evening's revelry.

It was alleged that everyone in Hollywood except Greta Garbo had visited the Brown Derby. The modest menu of corned beef hash, stew, pot roast and pie drew raves worthy of haute cuisine. The waitresses wore hoopskirts starched to resemble derbies, and the entire menage began showing up regularly in fan magazines and even in films as a result of Hollywood's narcissism.

Perhaps inevitably, the second Brown Derby opened in 1929, near the intersection of Hollywood Boulevard and Vine Street. It was twice as large as the original, and the extra hundred seats were in great demand. The menu remained the same, committed to simple food made with good ingredients. Low-sided booths provided maximum visibility, and in the early days the staff was all male: the fastidious Somborn inspected every day to ensure spotless uniforms and shadowless shaves. The first Derby had become famous for the caricatures of film personalities painted on its walls, and the Hollywood Derby hastened to keep up with its own tradition by putting artist Eddie Vitch to work. The maitre d'hotel was in charge of the resulting art gallery; his duties included rotating the portraits to make sure an exspouse was not adjacent to a current one. The movie crowd favored the booths, and the

management continued to page famous customers and to deliver a phone to their tables, as at the Wilshire Derby. The ritual assured everyone involved of his or her importance, and it was rumored that some patrons tipped generously to guarantee that they would receive the prestigious 'phone call' during their appearance at the Derby. Louella Parsons made her headquarters at the Hollywood (or Vine Street) Derby, and her relative, Margaret Ettinger, was in charge of the restaurant's public-relations department – an innovation that paid off in the form of a perpetual line of fans at the front door hoping for autographs and glimpses of their favorites.

Above: The attractive bungalow court at the Garden of Allah on Sunset Boulevard, where many film colonists took up residence before they found permanent quarters.

Below: The gregarious Douglas Fairbanks, Sr, is accosted by his fans outside the Vine Street Brown Derby.

Left: Douglas Fairbanks Jr, and Joan Crawford on their honeymoon at Catalina Beach in 1928.

Right: Comedian Buster Keaton, 'the great stone face' (right), and the handsome Gilbert Roland look unhappy about being photographed in the water but Norma Talmadge seems unperturbed.

Right: Norma Talmadge (right) and her sister Constance at Norma's beach house in Santa Monica.

Below: Huge house parties at the beach, like this one in 1926 at the vacation home of Richard Barthelmess, often went on for days. Bea Lille, Roscoe Arbuckle and Blanche Sweet were among the guests.

When the film community tired of the limelight, Jazz Age recreation was available out of town, notably across the Mexican border. Tijuana (or Tia Juana, as it was called) was only two hours away by car and just about everything was legal there. Fight promoter 'Sunny Jim' Coffroth popularized the wide-open border town with the film colony when he put together the Baja California Investment Company to open a racetrack there. Its 1916 opening attracted 10,000 spectators, including many big names from Hollywood, and when restaurateur Baron Long joined the investment group, satisfied patrons of the Ship Cafe and the Vernon Country Club knew that Mexican-American relations were in good hands. Meanwhile, a $10,000 gambling casino called the Monte Carlo increased the attractions of the once-desolate border town still further.

Wild stories of opium dens, gambling halls, prostitution and other forbidden pastimes brought a steady stream of tourists into Tijuana until World War I closed the border for a while. By the time it reopened, Baron Long had put up his Sunset Inn, an expensive extension of the Monte Carlo, on the route to the racetrack. The lure of gambling on Long's roulette wheels before they put their money on the horses was irresistible to big spenders like Carl Laemmle. Studio head Joseph Schenck was frequently seen in the appropriately named Gold Room: he and his wife, Norma Talmadge, had been known to lose $100,000 on a single race. Before the scandal that wrecked his career, Fatty Arbuckle entertained aboard several private railway cars on his way to the Mexican racetrack.

Above: The main street of Ensenada, Mexico, some 70 miles south of San Diego – a popular film-colony resort because of its unhurried atmosphere and beautiful bay.

Below: The palatial million-dollar casino at Agua Caliente, Mexico, which opened in 1926.

Tijuana had been a saloon town since the turn of the century, but the local watering holes were considerably upgraded with the coming of the film crowd. Jazz pianos and orchestras sent their strains out into the night, as dedicated drinkers made their way from the Last Chance Saloon to the Red Mill, with stops at the Savoy Cafe, the Tivoli, the Anchor Bar, Booze's Place and other points between. Main Street had the freewheeling atmosphere of a frontier town, and the local 'green beer' had an effect that one observer compared to that of swallowing a lighted pinwheel. However, he assured his readers

that 'The science of blending alcohol with creosote, concentrated beet juice, and faucet water has reached such a high stage of development on the North American continent that the drinks of Tijuana seldom cause death if taken in moderation.'

The prestigious Jockey Club formed around Tijuana's popular racetrack – replaced in 1926 by a much larger facility – and was the scene of many a Hollywood festivity. Silent film star John Gilbert married Leatrice Joy there, and Tom Mix, Buster Keaton and Lew Cody were regulars. The California Club and the San Francisco were both expensive, and celebrities like Mary Astor, Bessie Love, Jack Dempsey and Clara Bow braved Mexico's rudimentary roads to gather and gamble there. In 1927 the Foreign Club opened, with accommodations for several thousand. Roulette, *chemin de fer*, black jack and slot machines competed for Hollywood dollars. The Foreign Club's Cafe de Luxe featured a young dancer named Margarita Cansino. Film executives subsequently brought her to Hollywood and launched her on a glittering career, as Rita Hayworth.

The border's major resort, Agua Caliente, opened in 1926. It was an elegant and expensive spa that offered a variety of hot baths, swimming pools, gambling in the Salon de Oro (with gold pieces only), boutiques, golfing, tennis courts and a dog-racing track. The new Jockey Club racetrack held 50,000 people, versus the 15,000-person capacity of the old track, and nightlife with a Spanish accent flourished.

However, it was not necessary to make the

Left: An advertisement for the *Johanna Smith*, first of the great gambling ships to operate in the waters off Long Beach and Santa Monica.

two-hour trip across the border to find illegal activities. Just beyond the three-mile limit, between Long Beach and Santa Monica, was a fleet of gambling ships that advertised their attractions blatantly. The first was the *Johanna Smith*, formerly a lumber bark, which appeared in its new incarnation as a floating casino off Long Beach in 1928. No Federal law prohibited gambling, so the California statutes against it could be flouted with impunity if the ships stayed more than three miles offshore. Naturally, liquor was prohibited aboard the casino ships, but that could be said of the land-locked nightspots too. The water taxis that carried customers to and from the ships suffered little interference from the local constabulary (although some were seized on ground that they were transporting citizens to the scene of 'immoral acts'). In fact, there was no effective way of

policing the gambling ships, and their number increased rapidly. The *Johanna Smith* soon had competition from the *Monfalcone*, the *City of Panama*, the *Monte Carlo*, the *Texas*, the *Showboat* and the *Caliente*. All this appealed as much to Hollywood's sense of drama as to its appetite for diversion, and there was brisk traffic back and forth to the brightly lighted floating casinos. Rival gangs, bootleggers and bandits all got involved in the action.

Below left: The floating casino *Monte Carlo* was the object of a steady stream of water taxis that plied between Long Beach and the showboat's anchorage beyond the three-mile limit.

Below: An advertisement for the gala Christmas-holiday attractions offered aboard the *Monte Carlo*.

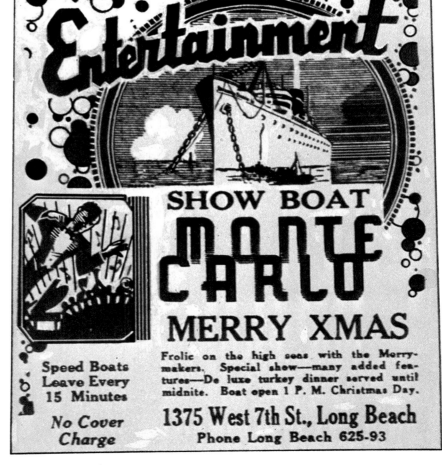

58

Not unnaturally, one of Hollywood's favorite recreations was going to the movies – especially to the glittering premieres that provided an unparalleled opportunity to see and be seen. Gaylord Carter, one of the greatest Wurlitzer organists of silent-screen days, recalled the Hollywood theater circuit for Walter Wanger in *You Must Remember This*. 'People forget that silent pictures were never silent. Even when they were shooting these emotional scenes at the studio, say, John Barrymore making love to Mary Astor in *Don Juan* (1926), there would be a violinist or a string quartet on the set. The music put the actors in the right mood. So in presenting organ music in the theater you were just amplifying what they were working to when the picture was being photographed.'

Carter began his career at neighborhood theaters like the Sunshine and the Seville in Inglewood; then his friendship with Harold Lloyd resulted in a job with Sid Grauman's Million Dollar Theater in downtown Los Angeles, where the organist described his first

Top right: Sid Grauman's opulent Egyptian Theatre premieres the Douglas Fairbanks swashbuckler *The Thief of Bagdad* (1924).

Bottom right: Founding members of the Academy of Motion Picture Arts and Sciences meet in temporary quarters at the Hollywood Roosevelt in 1927.

Below: Jimmy Durante, left, who would become one of the best-loved comedians in the history of American entertainment, with Roscoe Arbuckle, after he turned to directing, and Arbuckle's fiancée, actress Addie McPhail.

show. 'The picture was *The Temptress* (1926), with Greta Garbo and Antonio Moreno. The pit orchestra had thirty-five pieces. On the stage there was an atmospheric prologue with live performers *and* Paul Whiteman and his concert orchestra. That night Whiteman played George Gershwin's *Rhapsody in Blue*. It was the first time I'd heard it . . . All this for thirty-five cents if you got in before four o'clock in the afternoon. Incredible!

'Our biggest premiere at the Million Dollar was the original *Ben Hur* in 1927, which played six months and could have played six years. In those days a premiere was as big an event as a Broadway opening. Outside there were klieg lights and limousines and crowds, a bubble of excitement, of enchantment. Everybody would dress for the occasion, the men in black ties and tails, the women in stunning gowns. The stars of *Ben Hur*, Ramon Navarro and Francis X Bushman, were there for the first night. So was the director, Fred Niblo. And Mary Pickford and Douglas Fairbanks.'

After three years at the Million Dollar Theatre, Carter went to the Paramount, one of the largest theaters ever built, which seated 5500 people. Its great Wurlitzer organ had cost $100,000 and could duplicate the sounds of a complete orchestra, but Carter never used its 'thunderstop' attachment because of the experience of a friend who played for the premiere of *The Ten Commandments* (1923) at Grauman's Egyptian Theater. As Carter recalled it, 'A thunderstop consisted of a huge pipe thirty-two feet long, maybe five feet square at the top with a big reed at the bottom. The vibration it gave off was so powerful you can only compare it to an earthquake.' When his fellow organist used the attachment during the premiere of *The Ten Commandments*, 'The theater literally shook and rumbled. The sound almost cracked the pillars. Hundreds, maybe thousands, of people might have been killed. Sid Grauman was so afraid of the thunderstop that he had it disconnected.'

Hollywood's increasing self-absorption did not stop at the big public premieres. Growing numbers of studio tycoons and stars had private projectors installed in their increasingly elaborate homes so that they could entertain one another with their latest productions – a phenomenon that would become known as 'the Bel Air Circuit' during the 1930s.

By the time the stock market crashed on 21 October 1929, the silent era was over and Hollywood, like all America, had moved far from its rural origins. The original film colonists had found their new world long on scenery but short on entertainment. Disliked and resented by long-time residents, they had

to improvise a way of living that was molded and shaped by the exciting new industry they were inventing from day to day.

A major influx of European talent after World War I, and of Broadway stars when the talkies came in, had increased the sophistication of the West Coast film community, which both reflected and glorified the rebellious doings of the nation during the Prohibition era. Hollywood took fantasy to the limit, acting it out both on and off-screen in a decade that broke all the rules. During the boom years after World War I, even shopgirls and taxi drivers gambled recklessly on a spiraling stock market, and America was dreaming big. Affluence, power, personal freedom seemed within the reach of Everyman. Hand in hand with the new materialism and morality was the public demand for Hollywood's product, and the frenetic Jazz-Age tempo of the national dance whirled the film community into the 1930s despite the Depression that would soon engulf the world.

WHAT DEPRESSION?

During the early 1930s, Hollywood was riding the crest of the 'sound wave' and its streets still seemed to be paved with gold. If fashionable mansions along Hollywood Boulevard and in downtown Los Angeles were shuttered, it was only because their occupants had moved to the more rarefied atmospheres of Beverly Hills, Bel Air and Malibu. The studio system was in high gear; rising stars commanded astronomical salaries and spent them with abandon. Wall Street bankers were pulling the strings, and censorship and the glare of publicity put new restrictions on unorthodox living arrangements. But Hollywood repackaged itself with the emphasis on Glamour and swung into the Depression years with few signs of distress.

New nightspots came on line as old ones went out of style. The Brown Derbys and the Cocoanut Grove retained their status, but the beach communities – Venice and Ocean Park – were going out of style. Eddie Brandstatter's Embassy Club, next door to the Montmartre on Hollywood Boulevard, shot into the limelight with an exclusive policy that limited membership to a select 300

celebrities. Its Board of Directors included Marion Davies, Gloria Swanson, Bebe Daniels, Betty Compson, Norma Talmadge, Constance Talmadge, John Gilbert and King Vidor. The Embassy's unlikely blend of Spanish and Byzantine decor was considered the *dernier cri*, and the rooftop promenade and glassed-in lounge were hotly contested for private parties. Opening night was marred by the fact that fashion guru Howard Greer had supplied seven female stars with identical slinky black gowns, but all rose to the occasion and made a good joke of it. Before long, however, the club's exclusivity became its undoing. Film stars soon tired of parading without the audience of an adoring public and took their activities elsewhere.

Gambling remained as popular as ever, in settings that ranged from makeshift sheds on Santa Monica Boulevard to the Golden Club, where evening dress was required for admittance. The tract between Hollywood and Beverly Hills was filling up with nightclubs and roadhouses: its section of Sunset Boulevard – the Strip – would soon be synonymous with excitement and affluence. The first

Previous pages: William Powell, Mervyn Le Roy, Ginger Rogers and Chico Marx celebrate the opening of the Little Club at the Ambassador Hotel – 1932.

Below: Spacious Hollywood Boulevard looks anything but depressed during the 1930s. In the left foreground is Grauman's Chinese Theatre.

Left: La Bohème enlivened Sunset Boulevard in the early 1930s, with pre-Repeal drinking and gambling downstairs. Later this site would be occupied by the Trocadero.

establishment in the new enclave west of Hollywood was Maxine's, which was bordered by avocado groves and poinsettia fields when it opened at number 9103 Sunset Boulevard. Soon afterward, the Montgomery family, which owned over 200 acres along the Strip, put up four buildings in Georgian style. One of them became the popular Russian Eagle, a stylish dining spot that reopened on Vine Street after a 1930 fire. Three blocks from the original Eagle was La Boheme, with its cellar well stocked with pre-Repeal booze and a lively gambling operation downstairs. This club was soon joined by many others, as Sunset Strip was an access route from downtown Hollywood to Beverly Hills, well traveled by studio stars and executives. Agents began to rent offices there because of the convenient location, and the Strip really took off when Billy Wilkerson's Cafe Trocadero opened on the former site of the La Boheme in 1934.

The Frisky Pom Pom Club on Santa Monica Boulevard offered a Folies Bergère Revue advertised as 'Glorifying Hollywood's most Beautiful Girls.' The club's biggest event of the year was its Parisian show on New Year's Eve – featuring a giant egg that opened to reveal a diminutive dancer dressed as a chick, who went into her Mardi Gras dance routine.

Miniature golf had a big vogue in the early 1930s. Movie exhibitors complained that it was hurting their revenues, but Hollywood stars jumped on the bandwagon as Tom Thumb golf courses sprang up all over town. Faces to watch were those of Marlene Dietrich, (who would popularize the daring style of slacks for women almost overnight), Clark Gable, Jean Harlow and Maurice Chevalier, who had just arrived from Europe. In 1933 the commodious El Patio Ballroom became the Rainbow Gardens with the addi-

tion of Colortrope – 6000 colored lightbulbs synchronized to the dance band's music. RKO gave a post-premiere party called the King Kong Frolic in this unlikely setting, where orange and yellow colors accompanied a fox trot and red pulsed in time with the jazz tunes.

The Club New Yorker at Hollywood Boulevard and McCadden Place replaced the Greenwich Village Cafe and was especially popular with homesick Easterners. The Blossom Room at the Hollywood Roosevelt had achieved distinction in 1928, the year after it opened, when it hosted the first Academy Awards Banquet. Its modern ballroom was a good place for stargazing. Eddie Brandstatter opened his elegant new Sardi's in 1932, on Hollywood Boulevard near Vine Street. It was an immediate hit. Architect Rudolph Schindler had designed the cafe in contemporary style, with a striking facade of

Below: Johnny Mack Brown, Marion Nixon, Gene Raymond and John Lodge sample the haute cuisine offered by the Russian Eagle Cafe.

metal and frosted glass surmounted by the restaurant's name in futuristic letters. The emphasis was on lunch and dinner, which put Sardi's into direct competition with the Montmartre and the Vine Street Derby. Bands and live entertainment gave place to chrome-studded, stainless steel interiors and elegant daytime dining. Beyond the counter section adjacent to the entrance, Sardi's dining room was divided into two levels; discreet alcoves sported indirect lighting and the now-familiar caricatures of Hollywood stars.

By 1932 some segments of Hollywood were beginning to feel the effects of the Depression, but financial woes were offset by the imminent legalization of drinking. Local law enforcement officers were still staging the occasional raid, and some marginal clubs closed up, but most seemed Depression-proof right up to Repeal. The regular round of foldings and openings was dictated more by novelty and fashion than by lack of a well-heeled clientele. The Mayfair Club Balls, modeled on similar functions in New York and London, were private affairs held first at the Biltmore and later at the Beverly Wilshire and Victor Hugo. Los Angeles society was dominated by the select 300 who comprised the industry-only Mayfair list. The fiery Lupe Velez, known as the 'Mexican Spitfire,'

Above: The stylish Club New Yorker featured the Hollywood version of art deco.

Right: The Blossom Room at the Hotel Roosevelt was the scene of the first Academy Awards Banquet. Its modern ballroom was a popular nighttime rendezvous for most of the Glamour Years.

ushered in the New Year of 1932 at a Mayfair Ball with Randolph Scott. Clark Gable and Carole Lombard got serious at a Mayfair Ball where Mary Pickford appeared in a fortune's worth of jewels. The year 1933 brought – at last – Repeal, and press photographers mobbed the Beverly Wilshire to demand pictures of the December Ball, but the Mayfair directors stuck to their policy of 'no publicity.' The most determined newshounds stayed outside till dawn to snap tired revelers as they left the ball.

Even those who were not so immune to financial woes as the Mayfair set found plenty to celebrate in 1933, despite the fact that movie attendance had fallen off and some studios had to cut personnel. Gangster movies were the order of the day, and stars like Edward G Robinson and Jimmy Cagney could be seen at the Colony Club, whose gambling drew irate criticism from Los Angeles city fathers. The newspapers reported regularly that stars like Gary Cooper, Kay Francis, Jean Harlow and Lillyan Tashman were rolling illegal dice there. Finally, sufficient pressure was brought to bear to close the West Hollywood branch, but it soon reopened in Culver City, next to the Hillcrest Country Club. Two men with dubious reputations were in charge of the new operation. One of them, Al Wertheimer, formerly of Detroit, had been the moving force behind a new casino in Palm Springs, the Dunes, which opened a week before the transplanted Colony. Al and his brother Lou were reportedly part of the notorious 'Purple Gang,' but the Colony's clientele didn't seem discouraged by the rumors of mob connections – 3000 movie people turned out for the opening. Local residents were less sanguine. They lodged loud complaints about the noise and traffic generated by the undesirable new neighbor, which set off a round of raids in Culver City and the adjoining Southland. La Casa Madrid, in West Hollywood, was a casualty of the crackdown, as 400 patrons watched the sheriff's men seize gaming tables and arrest the management. (The band played 'The Last Roundup' by way of accompaniment.) It was reported that the guests included 'fashionably gowned motion picture actresses and their tuxedo-clad escorts, as well as society matrons.'

On the New Year's Eve before Repeal, the Club Ballyhoo opened on Sunset Strip. Billed as the Strip's 'newest and smartest cafe,' it featured Eddie South and his International Orchestra and offered a revue and dinner as part of the $5.00 cover charge. Around the corner was the newly opened Hollywood Barn, where owner Buddy Fisher and his Great Band alternated with Lester Montgomery's Barnyard Frolics Revue. The Revue

featured radio's Crocket Mountaineers along with Hannah, the Prize Cow, and Foster's Animal Circus. (Ten years later the Barn building would be converted into the famous Hollywood Canteen.)

Les Moore's New Frolics on Washington Boulevard featured the familiar chorus girls doing their all-night dance, with the bonus of breakfast for those who weathered the New Year's Eve celebration. At the Frolics it lasted for two days.

In the spring of 1933, Mae West's *She Done Him Wrong* stirred up a storm of censorship,

Above: When it opened in 1932, Sardi's was acclaimed as the last word in contemporary chic. It became a synonym for Hollywood's exciting night life.

Below: Les Moore's New Frolics offered non-stop chorus girls, drinks and dancing to its Hollywood clientele including, from left, Toshia Mori, Allen Dinehart and Mozelle Brittane.

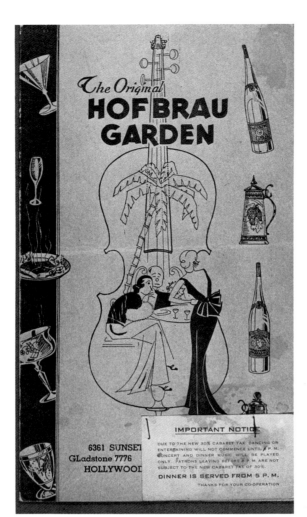

Right: The Hofbrau Garden at Sunset and Vine touched off a short-lived craze for German beer gardens complete with sauerbraten and apple kuchen.

Below: Jimmy Grier and his orchestra headline at the popular Biltmore Bowl in the mid-1930s.

and Hollywood nightclubs were the first objective of the clean-up campaign that ensued. Owners had to fall back on bribery to keep their operations going through a series of well-publicized raids directed at gambling operations and female impersonators. Beer permits were issued beginning in April, and the underworld moved in to offer 'protection' at $15.00 per month, guaranteeing that beer shipments would be delivered and not high-jacked. That May, Billy Wilkerson, owner of *The Hollywood Reporter*, defied racketeers and the Depression to open The Vendome at 6666 Sunset Boulevard, opposite his newspaper office. The new restaurant-cum-nightclub was originally designed as a gourmet shop that would offer a wide range of imported delicacies to 'the royalty of the screen.' Full-page ads in the *Reporter* kept Hollywood posted on the arrival of Westphalian hams, sturgeon caviar, paté, brandied fruits and other sumptuous groceries from overseas. A luncheon menu was added, and the Vendome became the only place to lunch.

As a fringe benefit, Vendome patrons were assured of being mentioned in Wilkerson's gossip columns. When a prominent socialite held a costume ball with an English motif at the Vendome, its stock rose still higher. The restaurant was soon crowded with people like Mae West, Joan Crawford, the Gables and Marlene Dietrich and with the legion of fan-

magazine-writers and newspaper columnists who chronicled their doings. It was at the Vendome that Louella Parsons picked up the hottest news item of the day – Mary Pickford's impending divorce from Douglas Fairbanks Sr.

The Hofbrau Gardens opened on Sunset near Vine, complete with dirndl-skirted waitresses and a militant brass band. The owner was a Swiss, and the restaurant was described (loosely) as Viennese with Swiss influence. Tree branches covered the ceiling, and hanging birdhouses completed the illusion of an outdoor setting. Shelves were lined with the obligatory steins, and Swiss chalets attached to the walls had Alpine murals in the windows. Swiss chef John Cley offered incomparable sauerbraten, Koenigsberger klops, badisher hecht and apple kuchen, and the Hofbrau was an immediate hit.

The night before Repeal was celebrated by an all-night party at the Beverly Wilshire's Gold Room, where direct election returns from the six deciding states were broadcast in a countdown to 'the peoples' victory over prohibition.' The Vendome, the Colony and the Clover offered standing room only for the celebration. Club Airport Gardens in Glendale, near the new airport, drew crowds for four days. The result was renewed complaints from irate neighbors and another round of closings and reopenings.

The auspicious New Year of 1934 was ushered in by a round of private parties and a wholesale migration to Caliente that included director Raoul Walsh, Bruce Cabot and 'the King' – Clark Gable. A few weeks later, the *Hollywood Reporter* announced that the Mills Brothers and Guy Lombardo were in town, along with Gene Austin at the Clover Club. The fleet of gambling ships anchored off the coast was doing a big business, but as writer Basil Woon described the scene, 'It doesn't always pay to be a winner on one of these boats.' One successful gambler was so laden with silver dollars that he sank without a trace when his home-bound motorboat collided with another.

The Colony was finally forced out of Culver City, only to reopen in March on Alta Loma Way. It took over a 26-room mansion in the English manor style that commanded spectacular views of the glowing city below – one of several gambling clubs disguised as private houses. Drinking and gaming went on unabated, while entrepreneurs closer to town plotted to bring their clientele back to the big hotels. Baron Long returned from Caliente to take over the Biltmore Hotel, where he opened a grandiose new entertainment room in what had been the Sala de Oro Ballroom. Architect Wayne McAllister came up with a design that furnished a clear view of the dance

floor and bandstand to each of 1200 patrons. No posts or columns obtruded on the 140-foot-long expanse of the newly created Biltmore Bowl, which offered the popular sounds of Jimmy Griers and Hal Roberts. Los Angeles society vied with the film crowd to reserve space for parties, and the college set took over on Friday nights. The room's notoriety increased with its national broadcasts by Station KFI, and it became the showpiece of the hotel.

Another new spot was the outdoor beer garden at the Gaiety Cafe, opposite the Pantages Theater. The Bohemiam Gardens opened downtown, across from the old Selig movie zoo, with outdoor drinking and a floor show. Second only to the beer-garden trend was the popularity of ice hockey games at the

Above: Louis B Mayer, center, presides over a festive group at the Biltmore Bowl during a benefit hosted by MGM director W S Van Dyke. On Mayer's right is Myrna Loy. Left of him are Della Lind, Arthur Hornblow and Mary McCord.

Below: Helen Vinsant, left, and Diane Corday are royally entertained at Agua Caliente by a visiting dignitary from Iran.

Right: Gilbert Roland (left) and Constance Bennett celebrate Halloween at the Trocadero with Clark Gable and his second wife, Rhea Langham, in 1934.

Below: Marsha Hunt and a very young Robert Cummings arrive at 'Hollywood's most popular night spot' to celebrate the completion of their Paramount picture *Hollywood Boulevard* – 1936.

Hollywood Winter Garden Ice Palace. The Russian Eagle flourished at its post-fire location on Vine Street, where Fay Wray turned out with John Monk Saunders, Marlene Dietrich with Josef von Sternberg and the audacious Mae West with her manager Frank Timmony.

Billy Wilkerson decided to capitalize on the success of The Vendome by opening a new place that catered to the night owls. La Boheme, on Sunset Boulevard, had just succumbed to its well-known gambling and liquor violations, and Wilkerson took over the club and redecorated it with the help of Harold Grieve, decorator to the stars. He redid the interior in the style of a French cafe and called the club the Trocadero. Press agent Myron Selznick hosted a private party before opening night, and the hyperbolic *Reporter* gave it full play in next day's paper: 'At least half the town must be recuperating at the moment from the huge and glorious party given by the Myron Selznicks at the Trocadero Satiddy night ... Among the gobs of guests were the Bing Crosbys, the Dick Arlens, Dorothy Parker, Genevieve Tobin, Hobe Irwin, the Sam Goldwyns, the Freddy Astaires, Bill Powell and Jean Harlow.' The official opening was held a few nights later, when the Trocadero was ballyhooed in the ads as 'America's most Continental rendezvous,' offering 'taste-thrilling courses' and 'two separate and distinct crews of Modern Melody Masters.' Outside was 'the West's first genuine Paris sidewalk cafe.' First-nighters sampling the expensive cuisine beneath Parisian murals included Joe Schenck, Joan Bennett and her husband, Gene Markey; Carl Laemmle Jr; George Raft; Sally Blane and a host of others. The elegant cream-colored interior, striped-silk upholstery and elaborate chandeliers were much admired.

Wilkerson was wise in adhering to a no-gambling policy at the new club. This gave it the status of legality: neither studio heads nor stars had to worry about adverse publicity, and the Trocadero was quickly embraced as a filmland nightclub par excellence. Jimmy

Left: Photoplay was there to record the arrival of David Niven, left, Merle Oberon, Lady Plunkett, the Fredric Marches and John Cromwell at the 1936 Screen Actors Guild Ball at the Biltmore Hotel.

Stewart, David Niven, Cesar Romero, Ida Lupino and socialite Alfred G Vanderbilt were equally at ease in the fashionable new watering hole, and the publicists knew they would never fail to find copy at 'the Troc.' The new club's popularity increased with the advent of Sunday-night auditions, wherein new talent had a chance to perform for the Hollywood bigwigs. Phil Ohman's band was the headliner, and soon capitalized on its association by billing itself as Phil Ohman and His Trocadero Band on sheet-music covers.

Sunset Boulevard was rapidly filling up with glittering nightspots, and the hills above it offered more discreet entertainment for those in flight from publicity – converted Spanish-style mansions like the Club Mont-Aire on Harold Way. They offered a variety of entertainment but did little advertising, depending upon word of mouth for their clientele.

Post-Repeal Hollywood remained avid for novelty and took an immediate liking to Don the Beachcomber, who began serving exotic rum drinks at a bamboo bar on McCadden Place. Chinese cuisine was an additional attraction, and the popularity of Don's Zombies and Missionary's Downfalls soon necessitated a move to larger quarters across the street. The new Don the Beachcomber was a rambling stucco building surrounded by a grove of bamboo and featuring an open court with live palm trees. Just inside the door was a Chinese grocery store, and shops that

dispensed rum, gifts and leis. The decor was pure Hollywood South Seas, with varnished monkey-pod wood tables and dim lighting for the Black Hole of Calcutta and the Cannibal Room. Bunches of bananas were available for the plucking, and water was sprayed from the ceiling onto a tin roof to simulate a tropical rainstorm. Fresh leis were flown in from Hawaii for presentation to special guests, who also had their personal chopsticks available in a special case. A velvet rope had to be installed to restrain the crowds that gathered to sample the Shark's Tooth, the

Below: Ida Lupino and Louis Hayward share one of the dime-sized cocktail tables at the Trocadero.

The fiery Mexican actress Lupe Velez, seen here with Johnny Weissmuller of *Tarzan* fame, was a fixture of the 1930s party circuit.

Right: The glamorous Marlene Dietrich appeared as a swan at an elegant costume party hosted by the Countess di Frasso, a tireless party-giver, at her Coldwater Canyon mansion.

Never Say Die and the now-familiar Zombie (originally invented as a hangover cure). Joan Crawford, Dixie Lee and Bing Crosby, Rudy Vallee and Marlene Dietrich were frequent patrons.

Throughout 1934 Hollywood continued to seem immune from the Depression. Box-office receipts were up again, and there was no end in sight to the demand for Hollywood's product. The gritty gangster movies and grim horror films of the early Depression years gave way to musical-comedy extravaganzas and romances that catered to the public taste for escapist fare. Studios and press agents urged – even demanded – that their up-and-coming players appear on the town at the smartest clubs and parties. Established stars had to keep making appearances to maintain their hold on celebrity, that most ephemeral of attributes. One of the year's biggest social events was the Screen Actors Guild Ball at the new Biltmore Bowl. George Montgomery chaired the affair, with the help of Jimmy Cagney and Joe E Brown. The evening coincided with Warner Bros.' premiere of the highly touted *Flirtation Walk* (1934), at Warners Hollywood Theater, and a glittering assembly danced the latest crazes – the Continental and La Cucaracha – far into the night. A month later, *The Examiner* would list the year's most popular stars: Will Rogers, Clark Gable, Janet Gaynor, Wallace Beery, Mae West, Joan Crawford, Bing Crosby, Shirley Temple, Marie Dressler and Norma Shearer.

The long-established Victor Hugo Restaurant moved from downtown Los Angeles to Beverly Hills at the end of 1934. United Airlines offered special Christmas jaunts to

Caliente, where prices were a modest $5.00 per night on weekends, including the Dinner Dansant. It was the spa's casino that proved expensive even to wealthy moviemakers.

The Trocadero maintained its status with the stars, who frequently booked it for private parties like the affair given by movie executive Joe Schenck to congratulate Darryl Zanuck on the birth of his son, Richard. Guests at the December 1934 event included Louis B Mayer, Michael Curtiz, Wallace Beery, Sid Grauman, Fredric March, Irving Thalberg, Hal Roach, Harry Cohn and Irving Berlin. By this time the demand for musicals had attracted some of Broadway's top composers to the Gold Coast.

The Friday night fights at the Hollywood Legion Arena drew an assortment of colorful characters, including Lupe 'the Mexican Spitfire' Velez, who adopted all the Mexican fighters as her protégés and cheered them wildly through every round. If the Mexican fighter lost, she would climb into the ring and physically attack the referee. Lupe and her husband, Johnny Weissmuller, were fixtures of Hollywood nightlife, who staged some impressive knock-down, drag-out fights of their own on the party circuit. Another swinger was Dorothy di Frasso, who had inherited a fortune and married first a British adventurer, then an Italian count. She came to Hollywood with his title, leaving the count behind, and took over a roomy mansion off Coldwater Canyon where she gave more or less continuous parties. The Countess di Frasso took a more-than-maternal interest in the young Gary Cooper, recently arrived from Montana, and frequently took him abroad with her on African safaris and European tours designed to make him more a man of the world. Later, she had a headline-making affair with a handsome young gangster from Chicago named Charles Siegel. 'Bugsy' Siegel, the Countess, and two companions took a four-month sea voyage together that ended in charges of piracy and suits for assault. An illicit cargo was allegedly delivered to Louis 'Lepke' Buchalter, another gangster whose career would end in the electric chair at Sing Sing. The countess assured the federal grand jury that she had merely been in 'the company of a good friend' and knew nothing about the charges. She got off free, but Siegel was shot to death soon afterward in his Beverly Hills home by an unknown assailant who fired a machine gun through his living room window.

However, gangland slayings were not the norm, despite the fact that many clubs, especially those with casinos, hired armed guards to protect their investment. Image-conscious as it was, Hollywood shied away from overtly lawless behavior in public – it

Right: Marion Davies was famous for her lavish costume parties, like this Civil War-theme gala celebrating the birthday of William Randolph Hearst.

Below: Joan Crawford and Franchot Tone fuel speculation about whether they have been secretly married, at a Guy Lombardo opening at the Cocoanut Grove in 1933. The secret was soon out. They were.

was too damaging at the box office. David Niven recalls that most private parties began very decorously, because a few press photographers had been invited. 'Glasses and bottles were kept out of sight and husbands, wives, and established "couples" sat close and smiled fondly at each other.' However, 'Once the press had departed, freedom of movement, speech, and behavior was restored, and the opportunity for all hell to break loose was welcomed with open arms and lifted elbows.'

Christmas, New Year's, birthdays, premieres, even divorces, all called for a Hollywood party. Some were annual events, like Marion Davies' birthday party for W R Hearst, Sonja Henie's farewell before her spring trip to Norway and Joseph Cotten's all-day Fourth of July celebration every summer. Gatherings could range from half a dozen couples to a costume ball for several thousand at one of the several grandiose Hearst establishments. Darryl Zanuck invited friends to ride his polo ponies through the San Fernando Valley by moonlight. Deborah Kerr spent her first night in Hollywood at a premiere party for producer Nunnally Johnson's *Mr Peabody and the Mermaid* (complete with disgruntled topless blondes in shiny green-sequined fishtails propped up against the bar). Basil Rathbone had 300 tons of snow trucked down from Big Bear Mountain at great expense for a Christmas party, only to have it turn to slush in a warm, torrential rain. The City of Beverly Hills was not amused.

A great many private houses had their own projection rooms, and 20 or 30 dinner guests were routinely invited to preview the newest films on the informal 'Bel Air Circuit.' Astute producers refused to expose their pictures this way, as the reception was often critical and destructive, but some could not resist the chance to show off their latest brain child. As the evening wore on, streaking and nude swimming in floodlit pools were not unheard of. Liquor was the main Hollywood 'high,' but marijuana smoking flourished at all-night jam sessions in dimly lit nightclubs and in some esoteric enclaves like Laurel Canyon.

The typical black-tie party consisted of 200 to 300 guests who dined on food and drink provided by Romanoff's or Dave Chasen and

danced on boarded-over swimming pools under striped awnings until the early-morning hours. Smaller parties were catered and served by a band of experienced butlers, the best known of whom were Marcel and Theodore. They arrived at mid-afternoon to take over the kitchen and relieve the host and hostess of all anxiety. Bottles, food, hors d'oeuvres and assistants appeared as if by magic, and impeccable service prevailed throughout the party.

Some Hollywood parties were given by wealthy admirers of the film comunity who enjoyed entertaining the rich and famous. Pasadena, Santa Barbara and Palm Springs hostesses vied with each other for celebrity guests. One shy and eccentric millionaire named Atwater Kent, who owned a grand estate above Beverly Hills called Capo di Monte, was famous for the elegance and expense of his parties, but many guests never even caught a glimpse of him. He usually retired to a big leather wing chair in the library, and only diligent search enabled one to thank him for his hospitality. Once found, he was touchingly grateful for the attention. In his will, he left bequests to 73 'friends' who were virtual strangers to him, enjoining them, rather pathetically, to use the money 'for happiness.'

Late 1934 saw the opening of the new Santa Anita racetrack in Arcadia. Polo fanciers like Zanuck and Disney secured their season boxes early, but many disgruntled race fans were left out in the cold, with standing room only predicted for the season. A popular party game of the time was Airplane. It centered on an imaginary transport plane that was doomed to fly around and around forever because some mechanical problem prevented it from landing. The play consisted of providing tickets for one's least favorite people on this twentieth-century *Flying Dutchman*. (It was even better if bitter enemies could be booked on adjacent seats.)

By now, tourists were streaming into Hollywood in record numbers, and the newspapers complained that the erstwhile village had become a big city. Studios like MGM were averaging a movie per week. Herbert Somborn's Hi-Hat Cafe (an upscale Brown Derby) had folded on Wilshire near Western,

Below: Helen Hayes, Robert Montgomery, Leslie Howard and Heather Angel following the action intently at a Hollywood Cricket Club match.

74

to be replaced by trendy Perino's. At the Ambassador Hotel, 1200 guests welcomed in 1935 in the Cocoanut Grove and Louis B Mayer entertained 70 guests at the Trocadero. The gambling ship *Monte Carlo* presided over a steady stream of water taxis ebbing and flowing from the boardwalks, and celebrants danced at the Casino Gardens to the music of Dick Sudbury and Tex Howard. At Glendale's Continental Club, Cab Calloway was drawing a crowd with his famous 'Hi-Dee-Ho!' Traffic in Los Angeles was hopelessly snarled by New Year's revelers party-hopping from the Cafe De Paree to the Club La Salle, 'Where Every Night is New Year's Eve.' Musso and Franks retained its loyal clientele, and the perennial Frank Sebastian celebrated 4015 consecutive nights in business at his Culver City location in February of 1935. A thousand-pound birthday cake was presented to Tom Mix, Monte Blue and Lyle Talbot as part of the festivities. Les Hite's band provided the tunes and dancers wafted over the West's first aerial dance floor. On Sunset Strip, Guy Rennie opened his exclusive King's Club, featuring gold keys for

members only and a champagne hour instead of the ordinary cocktail hour.

Motion Picture magazine enthused about the number of nightspots and epicurean restaurants available to the film community and offered its readers a pictorial tour. One stop was the Russian Eagle, where the elusive Greta Garbo could often be glimpsed in the far right corner near the entrance, dining on Beluga caviar. Mexican specialties abounded at La Golondrina, a converted wine cellar on Olvera Street in downtown Los Angeles. Satisfied patrons included Jean Harlow, Anna May Wong, Eleanor Roosevelt and Will Rogers.

Columnist Cornelius Vanderbilt Jr reported on the opening of Club Continental in Burbank: 'The most attractive salle was packed with as distinguished a crowd of luminaries as I've seen since the party at the Mayfair in Decmber. And it is truly a gorgeous room, formal yet *intime*. Its sloped roof is carved and paneled and tinted in shades that give it an air of respectability as well as gaiety.' Vanderbilt offered minute descriptions of Paulette Goddard's furs,

The popular bar at the Wilshire Bowl during the 1930s.

Colleen Moore's yellow chiffon and Mrs Joe E Brown's 'bird-of-paradise brown velvet toque in which she is certainly most effective.' He recorded faithfully that 'The party wound up at six, and from then until away past nine they gathered in little clusters at Sardi's, the many Brown Derbys, and the Armstrong and Schroeders, for a "supfest" (which is Hollywood's latest interpretation of the supper-breakfast combination).'

The summer of 1935 brought another gambling ship to the waters off Long Beach – the SS *Tango*. The enterprise was run by gambler Tony Cornero (recently released from prison for bootlegging) and manager Clarence Blazier, who took control of the business on a lucky roll of the dice soon afterward. Cornero eventually opened another gambling ship, the famous *Rex*, after leaving the *Tango*.

A popular novelty of 1935 was the Circus Cafe on Hollywood Boulevard, directly below the Screen Actors Guild offices. It was done in red and blue canvas, and carved animals cavorted behind the bar. The experienced staff had been recruited from the Montmartre and Palm Springs' Mirador by manager Frank Averill. Another theme restaurant was Omar's Dome on Hill Street, near the Biltmore. Its walls were decorated in murals from Persian literature as interpreted by Hollywood, with added touches of gold damask, purple velvet and a 52-foot mahogany bar faced in coral glass and stainless steel. The effect was, at least, impossible to ignore.

It seemed that Hollywood had more to offer every year in the way of entertainment. Even East Coast sophisticates who came to scoff stayed to marvel. A random sampling of mid-decade clubs and restaurants would include the Queen, an English bar-restaurant on Sunset; the Marcell Inn in Altadena, which hosted race fans on their way home from the track; Frogland, which offered – not surprisingly – frogs' legs to its Ventura Boulevard patrons; and Jack Dempsey's Nite Club on Sixth at Westlake. Lindy's was another popular Eddie Brandstatter eating place that featured steaks and chops. The Gay Nineties

on Vine Street, Jerry's Joynt in Chinatown, the Nikabob at Ninth and Western, Lucey's, across from Paramount Studios, all had their followings.

A scandal broke out late in 1935, when comedienne and nightclub owner Thelma Todd was found dead in her car after a night out at the Trocadero, where she had been the guest of honor at a party hosted by Stanley and Ida Lupino. 'The Ice Cream Blonde,' as she was called, had been well liked in Hollywood, and her cocktail lounge between Malibu and Santa Monica was a popular rendezvous. Todd had lived in a house overlooking the club, and the mystery of her death filled the headlines for weeks, until every lead and suspicion had been aired. The case was never solved.

A highlight of the 1935 holiday season was the opening of Club Seville on Sunset Boulevard. It was an impressive stone building faced in white, and its biggest attraction was the Crystal Marine Room – a glass-floored ballroom that made a sensation with first-nighters. Beneath the see-through floor, live fish played among colored lights and fountains. William Powell, Glenda Farrell, Robert Taylor and Jean Harlow were on hand to help

Above: Dinner was only $1.00 at the lavishly appointed Omar's Dome on Hill Street in downtown Los Angeles during the Depression years. Entertainment and dancing were fringe benefits.

Below: Producer Walter Wanger entertains Joan Bennett and David Niven at the Cocoanut Grove in 1938.

Above:. At the 1934
Academy Awards Banquet,
Gene Raymond, left, shared a
table with Leslie Howard,
Dolores del Rio and Cedric
Gibbons.

Below: The Cafe Lamaze, at
9039 Sunset Boulevard, was
in demand for private parties
when this picture was taken
in 1936.

inaugurate the new club, which also boasted a Circle Room for cocktails and an Arabian Room featuring dinners by Hollywood's top chef, Marcel Lamaze.

The New Year started with a bang at the newly remodeled Palomar Ballroom, now the Palomar Promenade. Exotic Arabian decor, Joe Venuti's music, the Hudson-Metzger dancing girls – all were included in the $50.00 premiere charge. At the Lido Room of the Knickerbocker Hotel, scenarist Al Martin threw a pet party for Hollywood dogs and their owners. Joan Crawford, Stu Erwin, Ruth Collier, Mervyn LeRoy and other notables showed up in elegant evening dress with equally elegant pets. (Two ambulances stood by to deal with possible casualties should a major dog fight break out, but the animals were on their best behavior for the event.)

A 1936 issue of a popular fan magazine offered yet another guided tour of Hollywood's tireless night life. Cesar Romero and writer Kay Proctor enthused about the cocktail hour at the Bamboo Room of the Hollywood Brown Derby. The Cocoanut Grove remained the people's choice for dinner and dancing, according to these experts. Next stop was the Club Esquire, followed by 'the Troc,' which was described as 'the most famous – and costly – of Hollywood's night spots.' Readers were advised that the club's drinks cost between 60 cents and $1.50 and included the 'Vendome Special Sling' in which 'the bartender makes magic out of ginger beer, cherry brandy, gin and lime juice.' In 1936 famous fan dancer Sally Rand (now 'all dressed up,' according to the ads) was mistress of ceremonies at the Trocadero, which remained Hollywood's number-one night spot throughout the decade. Its Cellar bar was frequented by Jimmy Stewart, Clark Gable and Carole Lombard, Myrna Loy, the ubiquitous Joan Crawford (with her new husband Franchot Tone), Robert and Betty Montgomery and Louis B Mayer. Just down the street was the Casanova Club, where a blue canopy covered the ceiling and the still-popular murals of Paris adorned the walls. Cleo Brown sang torch songs at the Melody Grill, where nightcaps closed out the 'dream evening' outlined by Romero and Proctor. (Its total cost was $21.55 for two.)

It was in 1936 that the Ambassador's Cocoanut Grove played host to the Academy

Left: Dressed to kill for a party at Cafe Lamaze, from left, Marlene Dietrich, Dolores del Rio and the famous 'fighting Flynns,' Lili Damita and Errol.

Below: The Hollywood Plaza Hotel, at Hollywood and Vine, had a major attraction in the 'It' Club, backed by Clara Bow. The club succeeded the hotel's Cinnabar, whose theme was film history, in 1936.

LIVE.. IN THE HEART OF HOLLYWOOD AT THE WORLD'S MOST FAMOUS CROSSROADS HOLLYWOOD AND VINE — THE HOLLYWOOD PLAZA HOTEL — IT CAFE — Rub Shoulders with the "WHO'S WHO" in the World Famous "IT" CAFE ★ ★ ★

Awards Banquet for the last time. The banquets had been part of the Grove's legend, along with the romances and the fights that broke out there in almost equal numbers. Ruby Keeler and Al Jolson, then husband and wife, were embroiled in a memorable fracas called 'the War of the Red Noses' when some boisterous revelers started a shouting and shoving match with them. Other patrons, waiters, even the band got into the act as the melee spread all over the club, which was a wreck before the fight was over.

The Ambassador followed the mid-1930s trend toward cozier rendezvous when it opened the Ambassador Lounge adjacent to the Grove, followed by the Fiesta Room, whose entrance was surmounted by a statue of Bacchus. The Roosevelt had already introduced its Cine-Grill, a modern room dominated by a montage of vintage movies. Red formica banded with chrome stripes fronted the bar and the bar stools resembled champagne glasses. Indirect lighting, chrome tube chairs in the grill and mirrored Venetian blinds completed the contemporary effect.

The Hollywood Plaza on Vine Street got into the act with the Cinnabar, which opened in December 1936 at a cost of $125,000. The ads described it as 'Breathtaking in its Beauty ... So Different in its Conception.' First-nighters were invited to partake of 'history in the making.' Anne Crosby and the Four Avalon Boys entertained. Manager Tom Hull unveiled the mural of film scenes that dominated the room, and special corners were dedicated to writers and directors.

New Yorker Dave Chasen, a former vaudevillian and friend of Harold Ross, editor of *The New Yorker*, had migrated west to open a modest enterprise called the Southern Pit Barbecue on Beverly Boulevard near Doheny. Ross had loaned Chasen $3000 for start-up costs, based on the excellent meals he had prepared for weekend guests back East. The original Chasen's resembled a lunchroom, with its six tables, eight-stool counter and a small bar. Chili and barbecued ribs that soon became legendary were available for under 50 cents, and the place was jammed with enthusiastic customers like W C Fields, Frank Capra, Buddy Ebsen, Jimmy Cagney and Pat O'Brien. Within a year, the Southern Pit had become a full-scale restaurant, with a menu of 35 items and a new room added on to triple capacity. The original complement of three waiters became a cadre, and the kitchen catered innumerable Hollywood parties. Chasen was a genial and well-liked host, and his parties both on and off the premises were always well attended. Later, Chasen expanded the restaurant – now known simply by his name – to include a sauna and barbershop. Homesick Easterners brought their friends to partake of the sophisticated atmosphere that reminded them of New York's '21.' Hollywood lore was enriched by stories like that of the day Bob Hope rode a horse through the place and the night that Charlie Butterworth, rather the worse for drink, tried to park his Fiat inside.

As 1937 approached, Hollywood had good cause to celebrate. At least 40 musical films

were in preparation for release in the new year, Technicolor was becoming increasingly popular, and David O Selznick had just completed *A Star Is Born*. New night spots were opening one after another, including Spider Kelly's, near Vine Street, which advertised itself as 'the most unusual place in the west.' The Clover Club hosted a lavish New Year's celebration attended by L B Mayer, Harry Cohn, Howard Strickling, Bruce Cabot and other industry notables. Harry Sugarman's Tropics, on Rodeo Drive, advertised 'No Couvert' and reminded patrons of its 10-year stint as the 'cocktail lounge of the motion picture industry.' Vine Street's autographed Famous Door was thronged by partygoers intent on listening to Louis Prima and other top bands imported for the holiday season. Other highlights included Ben Bernie's January appearance at the Cocoanut Grove and the formal opening of Victor Hugo's Garden Room.

In the late 1930s, swing was king, and the big-band sound was everywhere to be heard. Earl Hines, Ben Pollack and Jimmy Dorsey all appeared at La Monica Ballroom on the Santa Monica Pier in 1937. The Cotton Club and the big hotels offered the biggest names in swing. Other popular stops were the Avalon Ballroom in Catalina, the Club Alabam and the Plantation on Central Avenue, the Harlem of Los Angeles. The Palomar had been smart enough to book Benny Goodman in 1935, when he was still relatively unknown. Goodman sensed that his first-night audience wouldn't settle for marshmallow music, so he broke out an upbeat Fletcher Henderson arrangement for the second set and the crowd responded with wild enthusiasm. His month-long engagement was extended to a second month, as the Palomar broke all attendance records in the Los Angeles area. The new 'King of Swing' attracted many of the same stars repeatedly – Betty Grable, Barbara Stanwyck, Robert Taylor and Jackie Cooper, who sometimes sat in on drums with various bands. The Palomar's great size also made it a natural setting for such special events as the Hollywood Motion Picture Ball. It was the grand place to dance.

The popularity of 'Sugie's' original Tropics had spawned a wild assortment of would-be South Seas and Hawaiian restaurants. The theme's appeal increased as Los Angeles became a major departure point for the Hawaiian Islands, a newly discovered vacation paradise and the setting for exotic location filmings. King's Tropical Inn dropped its 1920s jungle look for a more glamorous Polynesian ambience. Marti's Club Hawaii featured a Paradise Room, Garden Lounge and Jasmine Patio. Joe Chastek invented a drink called the Tailless Monkey and followed up with the Zamboanga South Sea Nite Club on Los Angeles' Slauson Avenue, complete with the requisite palm trees, wickerwork and thatched roof.

By the mid-1930s, the Polynesian theme had been reworked in numberless variations and restauranteurs had to be ever more inventive in creating a tropical-paradise atmosphere. Rena Borzage opened her Hawaiian Paradise in 1936 to the squawks of live parrots concealed in fireproof bamboo thickets and the splash of two waterfalls cascading into a pond stocked with tropical fish, which sur-

Far left: Glenn Miller, standing, and his great swing band broadcast the big-band sound during a Hollywood hotel date.

Left: King's Tropical Inn, which started out with a jungle motif, switched to the newly popular Polynesian decor during the sophisticated 1930s.

Below: Joan Crawford, left, with Cesar Romero and Robert Montgomery at an industry party at the Cocoanut Grove attended by over 1000 celebrities – 1938.

Above: The Zenda Ballroom, at 7th and Figueroa in downtown Los Angeles, boasted an enormous dance floor. The orchestra, awaiting the evening crowd, looks lost in the vast room.

Right: Dolores del Rio and an uncertain looking Errol Flynn try the newly popular rhumba at La Conga, on Vine Street.

rounded the main dance floor. (The pond included a model of the island of Oahu.) The club's Lanai Room had a removable roof for summer and a glass roof for rainy nights.

In the fall of 1936, semi-retired film goddess Clara Bow opened the 'It' Club with her husband Rex Bell. The club took over the space formerly occupied by the Cinnabar at the Plaza Hotel, and it enjoyed immediate popularity. After the birth of her second child, Bow withdrew from active involvement in the enterprise, but the 'It' Club stayed busy at its convenient Hollywood-and-Vine location. It was lavishly appointed inside and out the long, luxurious bar backed by life-size figures from the zodiac. At year's end, the Trocadero celebrated its remodeling with a Big Apple Barn Dane, which celebrities were invited to attend in dude-ranch and farmhand costume. All the regulars turned out, including Betty Grable and Jackie Coogan, Edgar Bergen, Milton Berle, John Payne and Lana Turner. But the free-and-easy nightlife that had prevailed in Hollywood for several decades was about to fall upon hard times with a general clean-up of Los Angeles' corrupt administration.

For most of the decade, payoffs, bribes and bogus raids on gambling casinos had been the rule. A club owner who wanted a trouble-free operation simply went down to city hall or police headquarters and bought himself immunity from legal harassment. But in January of 1938, private investigator Harry Raymond was the victim of a car bomb while probing into municipal corruption; the fatal bomb was traced to a police lieutenant who was close to the mayor's office. Reformers who had been seething for years rode to power on a wave of public indignation, and the day of the phony raid and the payoff was over. The mayor was recalled, and the gangland element behind such establishments as the Clover, Century and Colony Clubs was pushed out of town. Nearby Palm Springs also clamped down on gambling, opening the door to Las Vegas, which would become the new mecca for casino operators in the decade that followed.

Even under a more stringent city government, however, new non-gambling clubs and cafes continued to open, several of them in the big hotels. The Town House on Wilshire Boulevard inaugurated the sophisticated Zebra Room, with striped upholstery and colorful African murals. A zebra-wood piano was set off by coral-colored walls and frosted glass pillars, and a neon zebra dominated the foyer. Then the Latin beat swept into town with the rhumba, successor to la cucaracha, and the Trocadero celebrated the new craze with a dance contest that attracted name stars like Douglas Fairbanks Sr and Jr, Marlene Dietrich, Joe Schenck and Dorothy Lamour. Shortly thereafter, La Conga opened its doors at 1551 Vine Street, between Sunset and Hollywood Boulevards, where a talking marionette named Chiquita greeted guests at the door. They were ushered through a Cuban-style patio into the main dining room, whose private booths were roofed with tile and surrounded by graceful palms. A revolving bandstand provided continuous music, and free instructors were on hand to introduce neophytes to the rhumba.

The off-shore gambling ships enjoyed a renaissance, as local authorities put the

quietus on land-based operations. The SS *Tango* and *Caliente*, anchored off Long Beach, were joined in 1938 by Tony Cornero's *Rex*, the most opulent of the floating casinos. After serving time for liquor violations during Prohibition, Cornero had returned to the gambling scene determined to go into business for himself. His entry was a former fishing barge on which he spent a quarter of a million dollars. Even then, it didn't resemble the sleek ocean liner pictured in his ads, but it did offer 300 slot machines, six roulette wheels, eight dice tables, keno, faro, off-track betting facilities and more. For

Above: The ubiquitous Joan Crawford, left, with Charles Martin and Mr and Mrs Charles Laughton at the Pantages Theatre for the premiere of *Nurse Edith Cavell* in 1939.

Blonde Betty Grable to become the most popular pin-up girl of World War II, clowns with Ken Murray and Mary Brian at the Trocadero in the late 1930s.

the opening there were full-page ads in the local papers and skywriters spelling out 'Rex' all over Los Angeles. Thirteen water taxis ferried high-rolling guests like Universal's Carl Laemmle out to the three-mile limit, where they could lose big money in relative peace of mind. The *Rex* did a brisk business despite local law enforcement agencies, who did not succeed in closing it down permanently until just before World War II.

On Ventura Boulevard, ex-vaudevillian Grace Hayes opened a nightclub in a converted barn that offered privacy from autograph hounds and paparazzi. Her husband Charlie Foy and friends like Jimmy Cagney and Jane Wyman soon attracted a crowd of celebrity 'regulars' who enjoyed the club's impromptu entertainment and friendly ambience. A host of 'me too' clubs was springing up all over the area, including the 41 Club on Beverly Boulevard, Billy Berg's Capri, Two Harrys and the Hi Hat.

Veteran showman Earl Carroll finally unveiled the lavish new entertainment complex on Sunset Boulevard that the Strip had been awaiting for months. Called Earl Carroll's Theater-Restaurant, it featured patent-leather ceilings, satin walls and over a mile of neon lights, along with '76 of the most beautiful girls in the world.' Ray Noble's music was another drawing card, and chef Felix Ganio was well known from stints at the Trocadero, Vendome and Waldorf-Astoria. Klieg lights lit up the sky as a fleet of limousines disgorged

Above: Elegantly costumed Basil Rathbone and Marlene Dietrich pose for posterity at a Hollywood gala in 1937.

Right: The young classical singer Deanna Durbin, one of the most popular teenage stars of the 1930s, shares a table with ventriloquist Edgar Bergen at Earl Carroll's Theater-Restaurant.

first-nighters including Bob Hope, Jack Benny, Jimmy Durante, Errol Flynn, Betty Grable, Claudette Colbert, Constance Bennett and dozens more. 'Broadway to Hollywood' was the theme of the evening, which featured richly mounted skits and tableaux showcasing Carroll's pageant of beauties. The new nightspot was so successful that it inspired a movie and ensured its proprietor a place in Hollywood legend.

Two days later, on 28 December 1938, another grandiose complex opened a few blocks from Earl Carroll's: Guido Braccini's Florentine Gardens. A six-course dinner was offered for a dollar, plus 'entertainment in amazing variety' in the Gardens' Venetian Room, ballroom, concert chambers and banquet rooms. Capacity was 1000 and furnishings were in powder blue and gold – not so elegant as competitor Earl Carroll's, but Braccini was satisfied with first-nighters' reactions to what he billed as 'The Evening Complete.' Gradually, the European-style garden concept was replaced by a more sophisticated decor, more chorus girls in less costume and a parade of big-name entertainers that would include Sophie Tucker, Paul Whiteman, Dave Marshall and Yvonne DeCarlo, whose film career began in the Gardens' chorus line.

The New Year of 1939 was cause for general rejoicing in Hollywood, where studio production was at its height. Such films as *Gone With The Wind*, *My Little Chickadee*, and *Mr Smith Goes To Washington* set box-office records and commanded international attention. Hollywood's prestige, power and wealth had never been greater. This heady affluence expressed itself in the film community's extravagant night life – clubs, cafes, revues, the Big Band sound, dance fever, cocktail lounges, opulent hotels and lavish private parties. The media riveted its attention on every phase of the film industry, especially on the public and private lives of the stars. As the decade ended, the legend lived on for the millions who were 'spellbound in darkness' by the magic of moving pictures.

Left: Showman Earl Carroll spared no expense in living up to the famous motto emblazoned on the facade of his lavish entertainment complex on Sunset Boulevard. Seventy-six statuesque chorus girls were featured in his elaborate reviews.

'RUMOR HAS IT'

As Martin Levin has observed: 'Movies were America's glorious pipe dream, and they were part of a double illusion. First came the make-believe of the pictures themselves. Then came the make-believe *about* the pictures and the players, mass produced for and by the fan magazines.' The public demand for information about its favorite stars led to the foundation of *Photoplay* as early as 1911, and the pioneer fan magazine was soon followed by a host of others. Within a few short years, no trip to the beauty salon was complete without a foray into *Silver Screen*, *Screen Book*, *Screenland*, *Modern Screen* or *Motion Picture*. Nor were the fan magazines the only source of information – or misinformation – about the personal lives of the stars. Up to 500 journalists made Hollywood their beat during the Glamour Years, and major personalities had their own press agents to keep them in the public eye. In addition, each studio had its own publicists and public-relations departments, which turned out reams of material on a daily basis.

At its peak, the combined readership of the two top Hollywood gossip columnists, Louella (Lolly) Parsons and Hedda Hopper, was 75 million worldwide. As a result, they wielded enormous power. Everyone in the industry read their columns daily, poring over every word as though their own press agents hadn't planted half the items with the columnists the previous day.

Louella Parsons became a journalist when movies were just becoming big business. She wrote for the Hearst papers, and her main vehicle was the powerful *Los Angeles Examiner*. Parsons' appearance was unimpressive – she was short and dowdy – but the power of the Hearst press made her courted and feared by the biggest names in the film industry.

Hedda Hopper emerged as Louella's rival during the mid-1930s, after a lackluster career as a chorus girl, then as a character actress playing society women in numerous films, before she turned to journalism. Hopper was tall and thin, a stylish dresser who was noted for her outlandish hats. Actors who hoped that she would go easy on them because of her own frustrated career were disappointed. She had an unerring eye for bad news – personal or professional.

When Hopper came upon hard times as an actress at the age of 50, Parsons took an interest in her, mentioning her in her columns and introducing her to W R Hearst. But a bitter rivalry began when a Hearst intimate asked Hopper to write a weekly newsletter from Hollywood for the *Washington Times-Herald*. At first, its syndication was modest, but when the *Los Angeles Times* bought it, the war was on. Humorist S J Perelman described the conflict as a distillation of 'sugar and strychnine,' as the two gossip columnists sniped at one another in print and in person.

Information sources that had been sealed when Hopper was relatively unknown began clamoring for her ear, and Hollywood found itself in a quandary. Parsons' legion of legmen in quest of gossip was joined by a new cadre of covert information-seekers – waiters, hospital attendants, servants and restauranteurs. The star or studio that released information to one of the rival columnists risked the wrath of the other, and the film capital was caught up in a zero-sum game of subterfuge, flattery and outright lies and bribes.

Previous pages: Fred Astaire signs autographs for determined fans at the Gower Street gate of RKO Studios during filming of *The Gay Divorcée* in 1934.

Below right: Star Betty Hutton, with Louella Parsons, looks over the columnist's newly published book *The Gay Illiterate*, modestly described as 'the story of a great American reporter.'

Below: Serial star Pearl White poses with a copy of *Photoplay*, the first fan magazine.

Left: Loretta Young, left, and Irene Dunne flank Louella Parsons at a party given by the Countess di Frasso, which *Photoplay* described in a 1938 article entitled 'Leading Hollywood Hostess Returns.'

Below: Tall, slender Hedda Hopper often played society women during her career as a character actress, before she turned to journalism.

Hopper and Parsons could jeopardize a career, land an actor in deep trouble with his studio and ruin reputations with a throwaway line or two. David Niven reports that everyone dreaded a telephone message that demanded an immediate call to Miss Parsons or Miss Hopper. But if the call wasn't made, a story that was untrue or damaging would almost inevitably run the following day without any chance to correct or deny it.

When either columnist favored an actor or actress, she was fulsome in her praise of their good looks, talent, or philanthropy. (Some observers say that Marion Davies' career was damaged rather than helped by the Hearst publicity blitz that attended her every act, including Parsons' constant refrain that 'Marion Davies never looked lovelier' in summation of a Hollywood party.) For the most part, though, Hopper and Parsons were easily swayed by the latest item from publicity-hungry press agents and their own paid and unpaid informants; their favorites were subject to change without notice. Unconfirmed news of an impending marriage, divorce or scandal appeared regularly, and if retractions were necessary, they usually went unbelieved. (One notable exception was the case of two major male stars whom Hopper accused of homosexuality. They sued for $3 million and won both a sizable settlement and a public apology.)

Although sophisticated observers questioned many of the items that appeared under the Parsons and Hopper bylines, millions of movie fans followed these accounts with credulous zest. Some critics publicly chal-

88

lenged the abuses of power that ensued, including J V A Weaver, in a *Vanity Fair* article entitled 'Tales from the Hollywoods.' He reported that 'There are certain deplorable meanies who claim that Miss X devotes her enthusiasm exclusively to those who offer substantial – nay, material – evidence of their affection.' Undoubtedly, bribery played a part in turning on the publicity spotlight. But the biggest factors were Hollywood's own narcissism and insecurity, plus the movie-going public's insatiable appetite for news about the film community. As Weaver observed in the same article: 'As long as those saps who can read swallow with avidity detailed reports of Rodney O'Toole's rise from bell-hopdom to stardom; how Albertine Loo uses sulphuric acid to keep her hair that exquisite hempen shade; and the home-life of Geraldine Gipp, who prefers the society of her chihuahua or her mother to that of the several dozen fellows upon whom vulgarians accuse her of bestowing a small favor or two – why, just so long will these knights and ladies of the pen shovel out the pap.'

In *Bring on the Empty Horses*, David Niven recalls that Hedda Hopper kept her own personal list of suspected communists, or 'pinkos,' long before Senator Joseph McCarthy became a *cause cèlébre*. 'Louella,' he adds, 'was a much softer touch, easily humored by a bunch of roses, but also erratic because she was apt to listen to the last voice before her deadline, and many of her scoops

Above: Hedda Hopper, in one of her famous hats, drops by the set of *Marie Antoinette* to greet Norma Shearer, who looks delighted – she'd better be. No one in Hollywood wanted to antagonize the film capital's gimlet-eyed gossip columnists.

Right: 'Lolly' Parsons had no trouble attracting top names for her 'Hollywood Hotel' broadcasts. On the columnist's left is Humphrey Bogart, on her right, Bette Davis, in a radio preview of Warner Bros' *Marked Woman*.

were a long way off target as a result. On one occasion she announced that Sigmund Freud, "one of the greatest psychoanalysts alive," was being brought over from Europe by director Edmund Goulding as the technical adviser on Bette Davis' picture *Dark Victory* (1939). This posed a difficult logistical problem, because Freud had been dead for several months.'

Both Parsons and Hopper were known for plying their subjects with liquor when interviewing them for full-page Sunday feature stories. The difference was that Parsons often joined her subjects in imbibing mammoth tumblers of gin or whiskey, to the detriment of her note-taking. Hopper rarely drank anything stronger than tonic, which gave her an edge on legibility. Similarly, both gossip queens enjoyed playing the devil's advocate for major talents whom they disliked. Greta Garbo, Laurence Olivier and Katharine Hepburn all fell under their joint displeasure at various times, without much damage to their solidly based careers. But two of their vendettas became famous in Hollywood annals: Parsons' attack on Orson Welles and Hopper's on Charlie Chaplin.

Parsons was outraged when she heard that RKO's forthcoming *Citizen Kane* (1941) was modeled on the life of W R Hearst and his protégée Marion Davies. She launched a concerted public attack on Orson Welles, the film's director, producer and star, on every occasion, and the Hearst papers refused to accept any advertising for the picture. RKO was alarmed by the adverse publicity: heads of the film industry even approached the studio with a $3 million offer to destroy the negatives before *Citizen Kane* could be

shown to the public. Fortunately, RKO resisted the pressure and released what some critics described as 'the best picture ever made.' Reviews were almost entirely laudatory, but Welles' career in Hollywood was damaged by the Hearst attack. While he was making his next two pictures at RKO, *The Magnificent Ambersons* (1942) and *Journey into Fear* (1942), a shake-up at the studio resulted in the abrupt cancellation of his contract. The new management announced that their slogan for the future would be 'Showmanship in place of genius.'

Hopper's special target was Charlie Chaplin, whose stature as a Hollywood icon would have seemed to put him beyond reach of such an attack. Chaplin was even more popular abroad than he was in the United States. (On location in France, he was pursued through the streets by avid fans clamoring for a glimpse of *Charlot!, Charlot!*) But Hopper took exception to Chaplin's liberal politics and to his continued British citizenship after 40 years of success in US films. When 18-year-old Oona O'Neill, the daughter of playwright Eugene O'Neill, announced her engagement to the 54-year-old Chaplin, Hopper's reaction was inflammatory. She was instrumental in instigating a paternity suit brought by a pregnant teenager named Joan Barry, whom Hopper sent to Chaplin's home with the message 'Hedda Hopper knows everything.' Subsequent blood tests proved that Chaplin could not have been the father of Barry's child, but the publicity tarnished his image in the industry.

Both Parsons and Hopper jumped onto the radio bandwagon with weekly shows entitled respectively 'Hollywood Hotel' and 'Hedda Hopper's Hollywood.' They had no trouble

Left: Publicity-shy Greta Garbo shields her face from a roving photographer as her embattled companion leaps to her defense.

Below: Charlie Chaplin became the object of a personal vendetta on the part of Hedda Hopper when he announced his engagement to the 18-year-old Oona O'Neill, seen here at the Mocambo with her 54-year-old fiancee.

Above: The fan magazines loved to photograph the stars pursuing artistic hobbies that demonstrated their culture and creativity. Here Douglas Fairbanks Jr is shown intently at work in his home studio.

Top right: David O Selznick, left, came under heavy criticism from the gossip columnists for 'insulting Hollywood' by signing an English actress, Vivian Leigh, at his left, to play Scarlett O'Hara in *Gone With The Wind.* Co-stars Leslie Howard and Olivia de Havilland look on.

persuading the biggest names in town to appear with them for free. Studio heads feared that refusal to co-operate would result in bad publicity and poor reviews. Parsons also talked Twentieth Century-Fox into buying the film rights to her autobiography (which turned out to be unfilmable). And her physician husband, Dr Harry Martin, was often employed as a 'technical adviser' on films. The good doctor's drinking was notorious, and David Niven recalled that he once slid quietly under the table during a dinner party attended by several of his patients. When two other guests moved to pick him up, 'Louella said, "Oh, let Poor Dockie get a little sleep – he's operating in the morning."'

Most of the crusades launched by Parsons and Hopper were of the tempest-in-a-teapot variety. Chaplin returned from a prolonged stay in Europe to accept a special Oscar for his contribution to the film industry. Orson Welles' reputation was based solidly on his talent and could not be done away by personal attacks that included his alleged avoidance of military service. The triumph of *Gone With The Wind* (1939) exonerated David O Selznick from the charge that he had 'insulted Hollywood by employing an English actress to play Scarlett O'Hara.'

Both Parsons and Hopper kept working into their early eighties – long after their influence began to wane. As Niven summed up their careers: 'They could not be faulted when it came to their devotion to Hollywood, and they tried daily to preserve it as it stood – a wondrous structure of corruption, fear, talent, and triumphs, a consortium of Dream Factories pumping out entertainment for

millions. Perhaps they did not do much good, but on the other hand, they didn't do much harm either, and it's a good thing they were both spared the spectacle of the once-mighty MGM in its death throes auctioning off Fred Astaire's dancing shoes, Elizabeth Taylor's bra and Judy Garland's rainbow.'

The studio publicists of the 1910s set the tone for those who would follow when they tried to create an image that combined the essence of glamour with a girl- or boy-next-door quality. Cultural embellishments were often thrown in for good measure. Thus silent-film star Pola Negri was depicted playing both the organ and the violin and sculpting – all in her spare time. Douglas Fairbanks Jr was constantly shown at work on one of his paintings. Studio publicists linked their biggest stars romantically, but mainly by innuendo: real scandal was anathema. There was a limit to what the public would let its favorites do.

Publicist Jimmy Fidler, called 'the man who invented Hollywood gossip,' came west to be an actor in 1917 at the age of 19 and 'nearly starved to death.' His uncle got him a job publicizing Sid Grauman's Million Dollar Theatre, and he was soon offered a press agent's job at Paramount. Fidler described his experience to Walter Wanger in *You Must Remember This.* 'The queen of the lot, without question, was Gloria Swanson. The king, if there was one, was Wally Reid. Valentino came later. But Wally was too much of a playboy to be taken seriously as a king.'

Later, Fidler went on his own as a freelance press agent, which he described as 'not a pleasant job. A press agent is a hound dog, the last one to be paid, the first one to be blamed. I had people who owed me three, four, five months, some of the biggest stars in town.' As a result, he turned to the fan magazines, writing articles and serving as West Coast editor of *Screenland* for a time. Soon after came a job as interviewer for the RKO radio show 'Hollywood on the Air.'

'I had everybody on that show: Jean Harlow, Bing Crosby, all the major stars. I had Garbo. I was the only man ever to interview Garbo on radio. Many of the letters asked why I didn't give news about Hollywood instead of just interviewing stars. So that's what I started doing.'

At first, Fidler had trouble finding a backer for his proposed radio show 'Jimmy Fidler in Hollywood,' but the idea caught on with a New York ad agency and the show began as a 15-minute spot with a 20-week contract for Fidler, who recalled that 'I cut out the interviews and just gave them Hollywood. I'd start with an open letter to a star or one of the moguls, do an editorial, and then do my reports and gossip about the industry. I also did the bell reviews,' (rating new movies on a one-to-five-bell scale.) The show was such a success that *Variety* ran a banner headline:

Above: Pola Negri looks soulful as she plays the violin to al fresco accompaniment, faithfully observed by a Hollywood publicist.

FIDLER DRAWS 255,000 REPLIES. Then William Morris signed him for $1500 a week, and Procter and Gamble bought his show and increased his salary annually for the next seven years. He also began writing a syndicated gossip column, at which point he was earning about $5000 a week.

Fidler stated that 'Compared to gossip these days, my stuff was tame ... The big

Below: Newspaper and radio columnist Jimmy Fidler, center, presents his 1939 selections as 'Best Bets' for stardom – Robert Stack and Maureen O'Hara – on his weekly radio show.

Right: Barbara Stanwyck makes the cover of *Silver Screen*, one of the most popular fan magazines – December 1936.

Far right: An idealized portrait of Mary Pickford adorns a 1920s issue of *Photoplay*.

stories were which *married* female stars were expecting babies. Today it's been reversed. Another big story in those days concerned who was getting married. Now it's who is living with whom. Actually, it didn't much matter what I said – the only important thing was to get the item first.'

While Fidler's show was on the air, Louella Parsons started her 'Hollywood Hotel' broadcast, which featured singer Frances Langford. Fidler, a friend of Langford's, got wind of her secret marriage to actor Jon Hall and called her to confirm the story 10 minutes before he went on the air. Langford denied that she and Hall had been married over the weekend, so Fidler put the pressure on. 'Louella listens to my show. If she hears on *my* show that her own singer got married and didn't give it to her first, you write demise to your career so far as 'Hollywood Hotel' is concerned, 'cause she'll have you fired in five minutes ... I'm only calling you so you can call Lolly and tell her before she hears it from me.' Langford admitted with a sigh that she and Hall were indeed married, and Fidler admitted, in turn, that he 'wasn't a nice guy.'

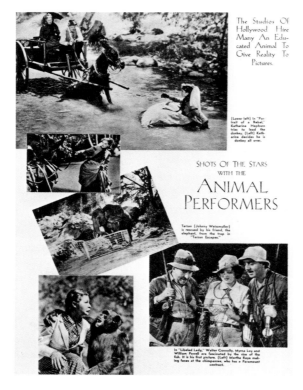

Right: Animal stars came in for their share of attention from the fan magazines, as in this 1936 feature from *Silver Screen*.

Far right: Reader interest and involvement were sustained with numerous polls and contests like this one for a Shirley Temple doll and accessories.

David Niven gives an amusing account of the way Hollywood news stories could be garbled in *The Moon's a Balloon*. When he arrived in Los Angeles after a disastrous scheme to popularize indoor horse racing in Atlantic City, he had almost no money but 'a sneaking feeling that I could make it as an actor.' Eager shipboard reporters questioned him about his recent activities, and he gave them a modified version of the rodeo fiasco. The story that appeared next day was headlined: BRITISH SPORTSMAN ARRIVES – PLANS TO BUY OVER A HUNDRED HEAD OF POLO PONIES. Niven's next exposure to Hollywood biography came when he was signed by Samuel Goldwyn and sent to give the studio publicity head, Jock Lawrence, a brief resumé of his life. Lawrence scribbled notes as he fired questions:

'Mother?'
'French.'
'Good, we can use that.'
'Father?'
'Killed in the war.'
'*Great*! What rank?'
'Lieutenant.'
'Jesus, that's terrible, we'd better make him a General.'

During the 1920s, no fewer than 26 fan magazines were being published to keep the public apprised of the Hollywood scene. *Photoplay*, in 1911, had been the first – it advertised itself as 'The Magazine for the 13,000,000 People Who Attend Photoplay Theatres Every Day.' Subsequent issues during the 1910s featured such articles as 'Beautiful California Homes of Movie Favorites,' 'Baby Pictures of the Stars' and 'What Your Favorite Will Do This Summer.' Then *Motion Picture* came onto the scene with the modest claim that it was 'the largest and best movie magazine in the world.' An early issue featured a seductive cover shot of serial star Ruth Roland and a feature on the Famous Players production of *Vanity Fair*. They were soon followed by a host of imitators, some of them printing reckless and damaging rumors along with the more innocuous fare.

In the early 1930s, the Hays Office began trying to control the excesses of fan-magazine publicity, in response to the filmland scandals that had erupted during the Jazz Age. The Depression had also put a damper on ostentatious displays of wealth and illicit or illegal behavior. Much of the 1930s publicity had a schizophrenic quality, as the public and private lives of the stars became increasingly separate. Posed 'at-home' shots of the silent era, like those featuring Mary Pickford and Douglas Fairbanks at Pickfair, gave way to pictures taken on the set, or at one or another

glittering night spot. The ritual of seeing and being seen in the right club – often with studio-mandated escorts – became as compulsory as showing up on time for work. Hundreds of couples who had nothing in common were thrown together into the publicity spotlight and just as quickly severed from one another. Serious real-life problems with drugs, alcohol, mental illness, or promiscuity were just as sedulously hushed up with bribes to the appropriate lawmen, hospital attendants, or would-be informers. But the rumor mill ground on.

Movie magazines also served as a means of direct communication between stars and their fans. Ginger Rogers confided to her public that she would like to be more of a homebody. Constance Bennett proved she had heart when she admitted to supporting 'four needy families.' Jean Harlow sent a boxed message to her fans in a 1931 issue of *Screen Book*: 'I regret more than I can say that my marriage with Hal Rosson didn't work out.' It was a dialogue, orchestrated by the fan-magazine writers and editors – a dialogue in which the envied stars often assured their readers that the price of stardom was high. Or

Hollywood beauties like Barbara Stanwyck endorsed a variety of products, ensuring wide exposure in national newspapers and magazines.

Right: It was *de rigeur* to be photographed at the wheel of an expensive imported car, and even better if you owned two or three of them like Joan Crawford.

as a memorable *Silver Screen* headline put it: 'In Hollywood, Health, Friends, Beauty, even Life Itself Are Sacrificed on the Terrible Altar of Ambition.'

A random sample of Glamour Years magazines yields such intriguing titles as 'How the Stars Spend Their Fortunes'; 'I'm No Gigolo! Says George Raft'; 'The First True Story of Garbo's Childhood'; 'The Price They Pay for Fame'; 'Tarzan Seeks A Divorce!' 'Can Hollywood Hold Errol Flynn?' and more. Recurring themes include money, love, health, personal history, marriage and divorce, studio gossip, Hollywood homes – just about anything that a movie fan might want to know.

As might be expected, wealth and its dispersal was high on the list of favored topics. The *Screen Book* article 'How Stars Spend Their Fortunes,' by Jan Vantol, informed readers that cowboy actor Tom Mix 'owns nineteen horses and three mules, and spends $600 a month for their feed and stable space.' This in addition to his $500,000 Beverly Hills

estate, a $12,000 annual expenditure for dealing with his fan mail and $1000 a year for white sombreros that the flamboyant former cowboy gave out to his admirers. The same article divulged that 'Constance Bennett spends about $15,000 a year to maintain her beach home and her Beverly Hills residence. Entertainment, clothes and pleasure trips cost her thousands of dollars each year, yet she lives on a strict budget and spends only what is necessary to maintain her position as a star.' Actors listed as paying annual income taxes of approximately $100,000 in the 1930s included 'Douglas Fairbanks Sr, Will Rogers, Harold Lloyd, Norma Shearer, Greta Garbo, Marion Davies, Ann Harding, Constance Bennett, Richard Barthelmess and Janet Gaynor.'

It was reported of Joan Crawford that 'Joan dresses well, but not lavishly, and manages to hold her modiste bills down to about $15,000 a year. She employs a studio maid and a driver for her Cadillac and shares a secretary and business manager with Doug' (her husband, Douglas Fairbanks Jr). Less thrifty, in *Photoplay*'s judgment, was Marion Davies, whose personal expenses were described as 'fabulous.' 'One can only gasp,' the magazine assured readers solemnly, 'at the lavishness with which she entertains. To attempt fixing the cost of one of her parties would be an utterly impossible task. Her jewels are insured for $500,000.' Another high roller was Wallace Beery, described as a lavish spender who was seemingly unfazed by 'the series of bank crashes and stock market losses which have wiped out the bulk of his fortune.' Even so, it was reported, the popular actor spent of $7000 a year to insure his expensive hunting dogs and $5000 to cover his gun collection.

A poignant letter from a Depression-era fan to an unnamed star requests that he agree to a lower salary so that the local theater may

Below: A 1936 map of Bel Air and Beverly Hills pinpointing the locations of movie stars' homes for eager tourists.

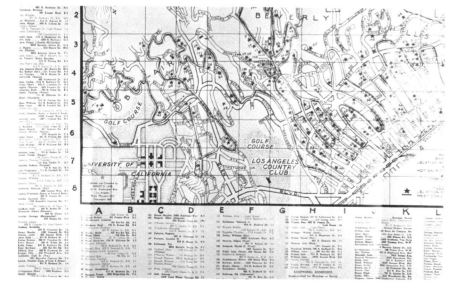

reopen. 'The managers said people wouldn't pay 25 cents admission, and when they charged 15 cents they lost money, even with good crowds. They said picture rentals were too high. . . . I don't begrudge you your fine salary, but with the closing of our nearby theatres, the only other is 16 miles away and charges 20 cents admission. Getting to the show and back costs at least 30 cents, even if we have no breakdown or blowout. So we can hardly afford movies any more.' The anonymous star to whom this letter was addressed replied via the *Screen Book* that he couldn't afford to work for less than he was getting. 'My relatives began the great migration to Hollywood when they first heard my salary had been raised to $2000 per week. Most of them developed strange illnesses that keep them from earning their own livings.'

Speculation about the stars' salaries filled many columns, and some personalities were not reluctant to discuss their finances on the record. Mae West told a 1930s interviewer for *Screen Book* that 'I got only $5000 a week for *Night After Night*. My new contract with Paramount, however, provides for a big increase. . . . No, movie money doesn't seem so awful big to me. When I produced my own plays, my percentage was often $10,000 a week.' It was reported that 'Wheeler and Woolsey individually get the same as each of the Marx Brothers – $100,000 per picture for the comedy pair, and $200,000 per picture for the fraternal quartette! Gloria Swanson probably refused the largest long-term offer ever made – $20,000 weekly. That was when she went into her own productions.'

Romance was, of course, the subject of

Two of the sexiest screen goddesses, Mae West and Marlene Dietrich photographed on the set of *She Done Him Wrong* (1933). West established her own deliberately anachronistic style involving heavy corseting, low decolletage and enormous hats, while Dietrich became a fashion trend setter, wearing slacks and tailored suits. Both women's film costumes were frequently created by the same designer, Travis Banton of Paramount.

Right: Carole Lombard and Clark Gable are photographed with their boxer, 'Tuffy,' on their San Fernando Valley ranch. The fan magazines reveled in the Gables' off-screen image of wholesome vitality.

Below: Barbara Stanwyck and Robert Taylor are 'surprised' by newshounds at a Hollywood theater in 1938.

innumerable articles like *Modern Screen*'s 'What's Wrong With Hollywood Love?' Author Katherine Albert blamed the high turnover of Hollywood lovers partly on the publicity machine. 'Remember the Clara Bow-Harry Richman case? As you know, publicity men evolved the idea of having Richman – who had not made his mark in pictures – rush Clara, who was a big star. Perhaps what you didn't know is that Clara was the innocent sufferer. . . . She was really in love with Richman and – eventually – he with her. But the roots of that romance were embedded in the soil of press agentry. How can love grow like that?'

Another obstacle to the course of true love in Hollywood, according to the same article, was careerism: 'All of the people in this amazing town have careers – and a careerist is selfish. He thinks first of himself . . . But love should learn the meaning of sacrifice and there have been only a few girls in pictures who, when it was necessary, gave up their careers for love.' 'Political jealousy' is cited as a third obstacle to lasting romance in Hollywood. 'When Alice White was a big star, and Cy Bartlett was the steady boy friend, dozens of people were trying to influence her against him, telling her he gave her bad advice, that he was a handicap to her career, that he was not working for her best interests . . . Most were trying to oust Cy in order to stand in well with a famous star.' The author concluded, rather pessimistically, that 'True love just doesn't have a chance' in Hollywood.

A *Photoplay* article by Kirtley Baskette, provocatively entitled 'Hollywood's Unmarried Husbands and Wives,' explored long-term relationships like that of Clark Gable and Carole Lombard (before their marriage) and Barbara Stanwyck and Robert Taylor. 'No hostess would think of inviting them separately, or pairing them with another.' The case of already-married George Raft and Virginia Pine was explored sympathetically ('Every effort he has made for his freedom has failed'), and the author also raised the question of Paulette Goddard and Charlie Chaplin: 'Did they take the vows on Charlie's yacht? Even Hollywood wonders.'

Ruth Waterbury's 'Round-up of Romances' in a 1930s issue of *Photoplay* offered to counter 'eyebrow-raising rumors' with the lowdown on Lili Damita and Errol Flynn, nicknamed the Fighting Flynns. ('Both claim the break is final. Is it?') Rita Hayworth's trouble with her businessman husband Ed Judson was blamed on Hayworth's burgeoning career: 'Once a girl gets really hit by stardom, it becomes like a jealous god to which she must, and will, sacrifice everything.' Stories of Rosalind Russell's elopement with Fred Brisson were hotly denied by Russell, although the interviewer remained unconvinced, along with 'half of Hollywood.'

Left: The colorful South Sea Islands menu-cum-map preferred by Don the Beachcomber.

Left: Ollie Hammond's Steak Houses used the map motif to highlight their locations and landmarks of the Los Angeles area, including the Coliseum and the Santa Anita Racetrack.

Menu

EARL CARROLL *Hollywood*

FRANK R. BRUNI'S

FLORENTINE *Gardens*   HOLLYWOOD

IT CAFE

1637 NORTH VINE STREET
HOLLYWOOD

THRU THESE PORTALS PASS THE MOST BEAUTIFUL GIRLS IN THE WORLD

★ BEAUTY SOUVENIR   EARL CARROLL'S VANITIES   *America's Greatest Revue*

Left: Souvenir programs from some of Hollywood's foremost Glamour Years nightspots, including Earl Carroll's, the Florentine Gardens and the 'It' Cafe.

Right: Searchlights probe the sky above Hollywood Boulevard at a Warner Bros. premiere.

Below: The Nat Goodwin Cottage at Ocean Park.

Bottom: Showgirls of the NTG Revue at the Florentine Gardens.

HOLLYWOOD-ROOSEVELT HOTEL — HOLLYWOOD, CALIF.

Above: The Hollywood Roosevelt Hotel, opposite Grauman's Chinese Theatre on Hollywood Boulevard. Its Cinegrill was a popular industry gathering place.

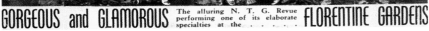

GORGEOUS and GLAMOROUS The alluring N. T. G. Revue performing one of its elaborate specialties at the . . . . . FLORENTINE GARDENS

MOTION PICTURE
DECEMBER - 25 CTS
A BREWSTER MAGAZINE

Lillian Gish

Fighting the Lean Years
see pages 28-29

The Smart Screen Magazine
SCREENLAND
March

NOW
10¢
7d in England

ALICE FAYE

CONFESSIONS OF AN EX-MOVIE QUEEN

WHY CHARLES BOYER CAME BACK

SPENCER TRACY'S HOME LIFE—WITH NEW, EXCLUSIVE PICTURES
Their Boss Tells On 2 Smart Girls: Deanna Durbin, Helen Parrish

The NEW MOVIE MAGAZINE
10 CENTS IN US
15 CENTS IN CANADA

MAY 1931

"THEY SAY.." EXPOSING THE WHISPERING CHORUS

THE LARGEST CIRCULATION OF ANY SCREEN MAGAZINE IN THE WORLD

MARLENE DIETRICH

THE PROBLEMS OF A HOLLYWOOD WIFE
Beginning.. THE HIDDEN REAL LIFE DRAMAS OF THE STUDIOS

PICTURE PLAY
JUNE 1929 25 cts

STREET AND SMITH

GARY COOPER
Painted by MODEST STEIN

Their Chaplin Complex

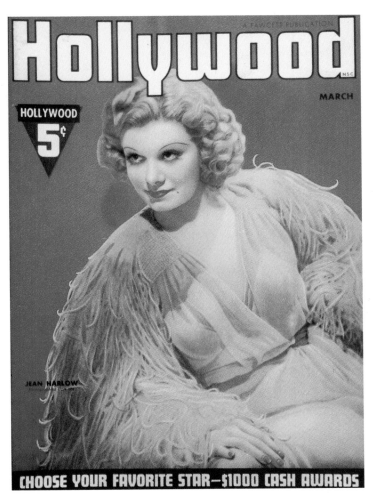

Hollywood

A FAWCETT PUBLICATION

NSC

MARCH

HOLLYWOOD 5¢

JEAN HARLOW

CHOOSE YOUR FAVORITE STAR—$1000 CASH AWARDS

LATEST HOLLYWOOD HAPPENINGS

MOVIE CLASSIC

APRIL

10 CENTS in Canada 15c

Joan Bennett

MARLAND STONE

GEORGE RAFT ..GREATEST IDOL SINCE VALENTINO

HOW MOVIE STARS FIGHT THE GANGSTER MENACE

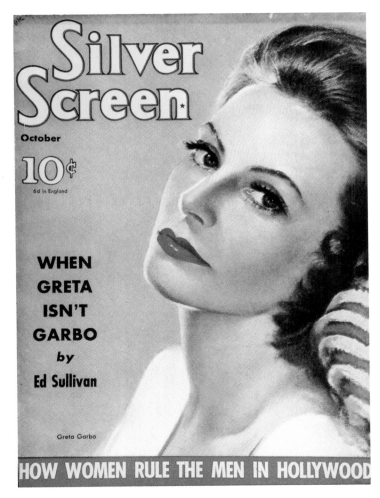

Silver Screen

October **10¢** 6d in England

WHEN GRETA ISN'T GARBO by Ed Sullivan

Greta Garbo

HOW WOMEN RULE THE MEN IN HOLLYWOOD

PHOTOPLAY

OCTOBER 25 CENTS 30 cents in Canada

RUBY KEELER

The "NEW DEAL" In GIRLS

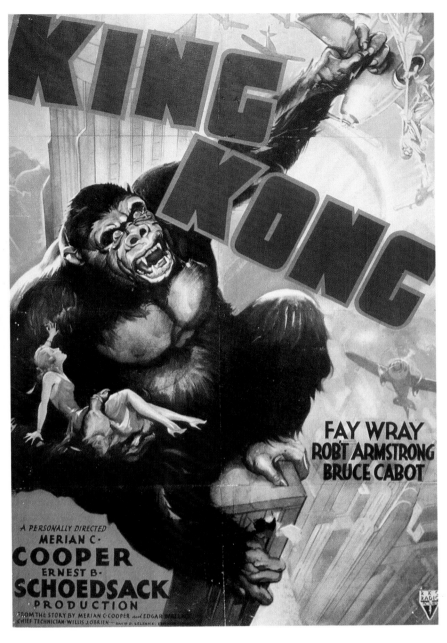

Theater posters for some of
the immortal films of
Hollywood's Golden Age.

Previous pages: A gallery of
Glamour Years fan-magazine
covers, each issue eagerly
awaited by a host of devoted
readers.

Above: The movies captured
the imagination of artist
Miguel Covarrubias,
inspiring the 1935 gouache
*Sigmund Freud vs Jean
Harlow.*

Left: The light-hearted
poster for *Flying Down to
Rio* (1933), in which Astaire
and Rogers danced together
for the first time.

Above: The exotic Middle East inspired two of the biggest films of the 1920s: *Son of the Sheik*, Valentino's last picture, and the fantastic Fairbanks vehicle *The Thief of Bagdad.*

Left: Screen goddesses of the 1930s: Mae West and Betty Grable.

Right, top and center: Hollywood postcards depicted the fabulous homes of the stars, including Errol Flynn, Rudolph Valentino, Clark Gable and Carole Lombard, and John Barrymore and Dolores Costello.

Right, bottom: The extraordinary William Randolph Hearst estate, San Simeon.

785. RESIDENCE OF ERROL FLYNN, BEVERLY HILLS, CALIFORNIA

FROM KODACHROME BY JUSMET

Rodolph Valentino's Home, Hollywood, Los Angeles, California.

830 RESIDENCE OF MR. AND MRS. JOHN BARRYMORE (DOLORES COSTELLO), BEVERLY HILLS, CALIFORNIA

1480-29

814—Ranch Home of Clark Gable, Encino, California

1B-H1015

Top left: The jewel-like Gothic Study at San Simeon, authentic in every detail. Hearst's agents traveled all over the world to acquire the art treasures for his magnificent dream palace.

Left: One of the many guest cottages at San Simeon, which occupied a quarter-million-acre tract overlooking the Pacific near San Luis Obispo.

Right: Casa Grande, one of the three great houses at San Simeon, which is now a California State Historical Monument.

Period postcards showing the burgeoning film colony during the early Glamour Years: from left, Jesse L Lasky's Paramount Pictures Studio; location shooting on the beach at Santa Monica; bungalows and dressing rooms on the Fox Studio lot; building a set at Metro.

Right: The studio that sound built for the enterprising Warner Brothers, who staked everything they had on 'talking pictures.'

"Stars'" Bungalow Dressing-Rooms at the William Fox Studios, Hollywood.

Building a "set" at the Metro Studios, Hollywood.

Hollywood's passion for memorializing itself extended to the colorful matchbook covers that collectors and souvenier hunters eagerly acquired from the film colony's night spots and studios.

Left: Joan Bennett and her husband Gene Markey before their break-up in 1933. The good-looking Bennett sisters, Joan and Constance, were highly visible members of Hollywood society, known for their fast cars and elegant wardrobes.

The September 1933 issue of *Screen Book* carried a story on Joan and Constance Bennett entitled 'Divorce! Is Connie Facing It? Will Joan Avoid It?' The Bennett sisters demanded a retraction and took the floor in the following issue to deny the whole story. Pictures of both stars were captioned respectively '"I am not facing divorce," says Constance Bennett,' and '"I welcome this opportunity to condemn the whole vicious circle of Hollywood gossip," says Joan Bennett.' (A subsequent issue carried 'The Inside Story of Joan's Divorce.')

The December 1937 issue of *Photoplay* published a stock-market style bulletin on 'This Year's Love Market,' which reported in part that February was a bad month for romance. 'Certain observers profited on the downside with the announcement of Fay Wray's separation from the writer, John Monk Saunders, and Walter Wanger's divorce from Justine Johnstone.' May brought little improvement: 'Luise Rainer and playwright Clifford Odets announced their separation,' although Joan Fontaine and Conrad Nagel were the object of more hopeful speculation. And June brought a major resurgence as reported in *Photoplay*'s inimitable style: 'All matrimonial issues shared in the most rapid upturn in months. Leaders in the matrimonial advance were Lily Pons-Andre Kostelanetz Nuptials, Frances Langford-Jon Hall Elopement, Inc., Gloria Dickson-Perc Westmore Knot, Virginia Walker-William Hawks Bridal Shares...' and so on.

The magazines often called upon the stars to give advice and counsel as well as personal details on their lives. Olivia deHavilland advised readers of *Silver Screen*, 'Don't Be Afraid of a Broken Heart,' and Douglas Fairbanks Jr spelled out 'Four Rules of Married Love' for columnist Dora Albert – despite his complaint that 'Writers write such mushy, oogly-woogly stuff about Joan [Crawford] and me.' *Modern Screen* published 'An Open Letter from Norma Shearer' which addressed the question of how much her marriage to Irving Thalberg had to do with her screen success. ('I've never attempted to use any influence which I, as Irving's wife, might have had – and all because I feared I would be accused of wielding a power I do not wish to have.') On her social life, Shearer confided that 'I love to go to my friends' houses for an evening. I love to have them come to my house – Sylvia Fairbanks, Merle Oberon and Alex, the Mervyn LeRoys, the Charles Boyers ... I don't care for huge parties. I

Below: The flamboyant and outrageously handsome Errol Flynn, seen here with his first wife, French actress Lili Damita, provided endless copy for the Hollywood press corps with his drinking, brawling and womanizing.

Below: No child star of the
1930s – or any other decade –
approached the popularity of
Shirley Temple, seen here in a
studio publicity shot with the
doll named for her.

seldom go to them and never, never give them. Sixteen is the largest number I ever entertain at home.'

Child stars were always good copy, and the 1930s fan magazines had a field day with Shirley Temple's 'Last Letter to Santa' and Deanna Durbin's longing to have a fudge party, just like any other 14-year-old (although fudge parties proved elusive when one 'has found fame and has paid fame's price'). Children of the stars came in for their share of attention, as in *Screenland*'s story on 'Charlie Chaplin's Kids.' Covering the legal battle that ensued when Chaplin's ex-wife,

Lita Grey, put his sons Charles Jr and Sidney under contract with Fox, the magazine reported that Chaplin 'was determined to keep his sons out of the movies. The famous comedian argued that he wanted the children to develop normally and lead happy lives as children. Acting, he intimated, is very bad for children at the impressionable ages of five and seven.' Lita Grey countercharged that 'Selfish motives are in back of her ex-husband's legal battle to keep Sidney and Charles Jr off the screen. She declares that Charlie has always been indifferent to his two sons and that his sudden interest now develops because he fears they may detract from his fame.'

Helen Twelvetrees confided to Sonia Lee her feelings about impending motherhood: 'Even if bearing a child means that I will have to retire definitely from the screen, it will still be worthwhile.' The star assured readers that 'Having a baby means that you can no longer be self-centered.' And Clara Bow, expecting her first child after her retirement from the screen, shared with *Screen Book* 'What I Will Tell My Baby.' A boxed insert by editor Roscoe Fawcett advised readers that 'Almost two years have passed since the name of Clara Bow was last featured in lurid newspaper headlines. In that time the Clara Bow of Flaming Flapper days has completely vanished. Clara today is a purposeful young lady who has retired from pictures – not permanently, as certain unfounded stories have stated – to become a mother.' And actress Joan Blondell was eager to break Hollywood taboos by discussing her five-month-old son with Kay Osborn, who published the interview under the plaintive title 'I Want to Talk About My Baby!'

'Studio Sweethearts' came in for a lot of attention, especially after actress Betty Compson revealed to a *Screenland* writer that 'I don't know what I would do without my studio romances. I have never made a picture that I did not fall in love with some man in the cast. None of these harmless affairs ever lasted beyond the length of the production, but I think all concerned enjoyed them thoroughly. Nothing really serious – just like the sailors: I have a sweetheart in every part!' Similar short-lived pairings included that of Lupe Velez and Lawrence Tibbett during the filming of *Cuban Love Song* (1931), when insiders reported that 'Lupe and Larry have it bad.' But no sooner had rumors of an elopement made the rounds than 'Lupe went off to New York on the same train with John Gilbert!' The same scenario unfolded when Velez and Gary Cooper made *The Wolf Song* (1929). A sadder case, by fan-magazine standards, was that of Loretta Young and Grant Withers during the filming of *Too Young to Marry* (1931). 'The kids eloped despite the strenuous opposition of Loretta's mother, and all went well for a while. Then it began to look as if Mother knew best. The Young-Withers romance went on the rocks, with Loretta getting a divorce.'

Above: The young Elizabeth Taylor with her doll collection made a strikingly photogenic subject for Hollywood publicists.

Left: Joan Blondell autographs copies of *Movie Mirror* for her fans.

Right: The marriage of Joan Crawford and Douglas Fairbanks Jr on 3 June 1929 was a popular match between two young people whose films captured the vibrant spirit of the Jazz Age. The couple appeared together in *Our Modern Maidens* that same year.

Silver Screen projected optimistically that the studio romance of John Gilbert and Virginia Bruce 'looks as if it might last. She was assigned the role of leading lady in Jack's picture *Downstairs* (1932), adapted from the star's own story, and Jack proceeded to fall in love with her. She is an entirely different type from the former Mrs. John Gilberts (Leatrice Joy and Ina Claire) and half of Hollywood is betting that she will make the temperamental Jack happy' (wrongly, as it turned out).

One of the recurring refrains in the two-way dialogue between the stars and their fans was the high price of fame. In Faith Service's article 'So You'd Like to Be a Star?' Myrna Loy described 'what is back of Hollywood's glamor front.' A cartoon sequence followed a movie celebrity through a typical day's routine of early rising, exacting directors, costume fittings, obligatory appointments, weight watching and retakes. The editorial summation was, 'So what? A newer star appears, and to you, Fickle Public, our heroine becomes – the Forgotten Face.' The

Right: Silent-screen idol John Gilbert and his third wife, actress Ina Claire, are captured on film before their departure for a European honeymoon on the *Ile de France.*

Far right: Heads turned when the sultry Lupe Velez teamed up – briefly – with rising star Gary Cooper during the filming of *The Wolf Song* in 1929. Columnists were hard pressed to keep up with the romantic exploits of the popular Mexican actress.

sacrifice of health to stardom was another popular theme. 'Fame imposed on Milton Sills the curse of nerves. ... He forced himself through picture after picture. Finally came a nervous breakdown.' Two other examples cited were those of Lila Lee and Renée Adorée, both 'in a remote sanitarium in Arizona fighting to regain their health. ... That exacting life, the rapid pace of the Hollywood colony, has sent many stars to hospitals and sanitariums.' Similarly, 'To his art Lon Chaney gave everything without stint. One role nearly destroyed his eyesight. Another left him temporarily lame. The suffering he endured in all of them undoubtedly caused this great actor's untimely and sorrowful end.' (Certainly, this was at least partly true, as Chaney endured real pain in his tortuous horror-movie makeup, including the vise-like harness that he wore for *The Hunchback of Notre Dame* (1923) and the spinal injury he suffered when his legs were strapped beneath him in *The Penalty* (1921). His dedication to these roles undoubtedly hastened his death at the age of only 47.)

When Hollywood went to war in 1941-2, commentator Walter Winchell was there to chronicle the event for *Photoplay-Movie Mirror* from his new vantage point as a Lieutenant Commander in the Naval Reserve. He reported that 'Robert Montgomery is giving the greatest performance of his career as a naval attache of the American Embassy in London.' Douglas Fairbanks Jr 'served as personal emissary of Mr. Roosevelt to South America and is now a Lieutenant in the Naval Reserve. Lieutenant Commander Wallace

118

Beery is one of Hollywood's best pilots.' Clearly, Hollywood was doing its part, with dozens of stars in the armed services and flag-waving war films like *Remember Pearl Harbor* and *Wake Island* being rushed through production in 1942. Still, Hollywood had its critics, including society columnist Cornelius Vanderbilt Jr, who contributed the article 'Why Fifth Avenue Laughs at Hollywood Society' to a 1940s issue of *Photoplay*. Commenting on a recent filmland party during one of his incursions from New York, Vanderbilt observed that 'All about me were the Four Hundred of

Picturedom, cellophane-wrapped and celluloid-displayed, pretending to have a good time. Grand people some of them, if only they would take time out to be themselves. No doubt in the depths of the modest little homes from which most of them emanated, they had for years been 'just folks,' the same as you and I [?] But once they'd made the grade to stardom and big money . . . the case was different.' Warming to his topic, Vanderbilt went on to say that 'The cheapness, the flimsiness, the gaudiness, the racket of the Hollywood social game paramounts anything anywhere else in the land. True, certain

Below: New York society columnist Cornelius Vanderbilt Jr angered Hollywood with his critical piece entitled 'Why Fifth Avenue Laughs at Hollywood Society.'

Left: A brief wartime reunion of stars who served in the armed forces: from left, Lt (jg) Robert Taylor; E J Mannix of MGM; Lt Cmdr Robert Montgomery, US Navy; and Capt Clark Gable, US Army Air Force.

Below: Commentator Walter Winchell kept all America informed about the doings and misdoings of the stars, and ruined innumerable reputations in the process. Here he makes his screen debut in Warner Bros' *The Helen Morgan Story*.

biggies are bigger than others, but the general run are pretty small potatoes when it comes to the bigger things in life. Each dollar earned goes out for so much nonsense that a Barbara Hutton or a Doris Duke must laugh herself silly.' One wonders how *Photoplay*'s audience reacted to this iconoclastic attack on its favorites.

For the most part, though, the fan-magazine writers and editors eschewed serious criticism in favor of doing their share to actively create the Hollywood style and character. 'How else would you know,' as Martin Levin inquires, 'that William Powell is a recluse who shuns publicity unless you read about it in four lavishly illustrated stories in four movie magazines during the same month? How else would you learn that Joan Bennett is hot tempered, favors blue and white in her beach house, and took Gene Markey from Ina Claire who married John Gilbert, who later married Virginia Bruce, who then married director J Walter Reuben?'

With the passing of the Glamour Years came the passing of the great fan magazines as they had been. As Levin points out, 'Communication faltered with the arrival of affluence, when the credit card and an increasingly gross national product seemed to make individual dreams more realizable and the big Hollywood dream superfluous.' But back issues remain to give us an insight into the days when 'The movies produced demi-gods and goddesses, ... and a movie enthusiast could extract limitless euphoria from the resultant fantasy.'

'MORE STATELY MANSIONS'

One of the first of the great Hollywood homes was Rudolph Valentino's Falcon Lair, on Benedict Canyon Drive in Beverly Hills. Responding to the new public demand that their idols live like royalty, and to his own past as a penniless Italian immigrant, Valentino spent a fortune on the property he purchased in 1925 for $175,000. It resembled nothing so much as a set for one of his famous blood-and-sand epics. The main Spanish-style house was repainted in taupe, with a red-tiled roof, and surrounded by a nine-foot-high stucco wall designed to protect his privacy. (Avid female fans regularly tried to bribe Valentino's private guards for admittance, or even climbed over the wall and entered the house in search of 'the Sheik.') As a result, the silent-film star built kennels on the grounds and loosed guard dogs in the courtyard and terrace every night – Great Danes, Italian mastiffs and a Spanish greyhound.

Other additions to the grounds were a two-story garage, with extensive servants' quarters upstairs, and a stable for Valentino's blooded Arabian horses: Firefly, Yaqui, Ramadan and Haroun. When privacy for riding became a problem because of his ubiquitous fans, Valentino almost doubled the size of his eight-acre estate by purchasing the adjacent property merely for the use of its bridle paths. Nearby were two friends whom the expert horseman could visit in the course of his rides: cowboy star Fred Thompson and screenwriter Frances Marion. Other neighbors included Gloria Swanson, who had a 22-room Spanish-style hacienda on three acres at North Crescent Drive and Sunset Boulevard, and comedy star Buster Keaton, whose new Italian-style villa in Benedict Canyon boasted beautiful terraces, fountains and sweeping staircases.

In addition to the requisite 1920s luxury car

– a custom-built Isotta Fraschini – Valentino's garage housed a French Avion Voisin four-passenger phaeton (painted his favorite taupe), with wire wheels and a red leather interior; a 1926 Franklin coupe; and a black 1925 Chevrolet that the star used for traveling incognito. There was also a 120-gallon gas tank to keep all these cars running and several uniformed chauffeurs to attend to them. The grounds were carefully manicured and planted with Italian evergreens and flowering vines. A circular pool dotted with water lilies made a serene oasis before the main entrance, and a pennant emblazoned with a stylized *V* surmounted the tall central tower of the house.

Visitors entered through solid-oak Florentine doors, richly carved, to encounter a life-size portrait of their host dressed as a Saracen warlord of Crusader times – with a young woman seated at his feet and gazing up at him. The foyer was floored with travertine marble, in contrast to the rest of the house, which was carpeted in seamless taupe Axminster wool. Draperies were of Genoese velvet or hand-loomed Italian linen.

The principal rooms were dominated by expensive antiques, which Valentino had acquired in Europe and New York with a cheerful disregard for any criterion but his own taste. Turkish and Arabian furniture took its place beside Florentine chairs, a fifteenth-century French throne with a Gothic canopy and an $11,000 Italian player grand piano. Thousands of books, with the emphasis on nineteenth-century authors like Victor Hugo, Dickens, Dumas and Goethe, filled the library. Valentino's collection of antique arms and medieval armor vied for

Previous pages: Hollywood's fashionable Laughlin Park section in the 1920s. At top left is W C Fields' home, at top right, the Cecil B De Mille estate.

Top right: Rudolph Valentino's foyer at Falcon Lair was dominated by this portrait of the actor as a Saracen warlord, complete with adoring captive.

Below: Valentino purchased acres of property around his estate on Benedict Canyon Drive to ensure the privacy that his determined fans continuously tried to invade.

floor and wall space with the books and furniture. In keeping with the movie-set ambience, there were elaborate period costumes for *Monsieur Beaucaire* and *Blood and Sand*, which the actor admired for their fine materials and expensive workmanship. These qualities carried over to Valentino's personal wardrobe, which set a luxurious standard even for Hollywood. The handsome matinee idol was a real clotheshorse: his dressing room closets contained 30 business suits, 10 dress suits, 4 riding outfits, 10 overcoats, well over a hundred shirts, 60 pairs of gloves and a comparable number of shoes, and 44 hats. Only at home did he relax in old, comfortable clothes, working on the engines of his cars. Even then he wore his trademark platinum slave bracelet. Other jewelry included a pigeon-blood ruby ring, a 12-carat emerald and a 40-carat sapphire, plus innumerable gold and platinum cuff links and studs, watches, cigarette boxes and scarf pins. It seemed that the 30-year-old star was trying to convince himself, as well as his public, of the truth of his legend.

Valentino's bedroom reflected his personal taste to a greater degree than any room in the house. Here the accent was on sleek Moderne, with bright, lacquered colors and crocus-yellow bed linens to match the star's dozen pairs of yellow Japanese silk pajamas. A built-in perfume lamp filled the room with fragrance when the light was turned on. Above

the bed, with its massive gold ball feet, was a large portrait of the Spanish dancer Señorita Gaditana, naked to the waist.

Despite all this opulence, Valentino's friends remembered him as a simple, unpretentious person, 'very much the Italian gentleman.' Lillian Gish recalled, after his untimely death in 1926, that 'His two great loves were horses and dancing. He had many talents; he designed riding clothes for

Dorothy and me, and he was a good cook.' To the end of his life, many of Valentino's friends were ordinary people whom he had known when he arrived in Hollywood as a cabaret dancer in 1917. Only four years later, the role of Julio in *The Four Horsemen of the Apocalypse* (1921) thrust him into the public eye as the great lover of the silent screen, and enabled him to build the house that Pola Negri called 'an enchanted castle suspended high above the rest of the world.'

Actor-turned-director Cecil B De Mille was on a shoestring budget when he arrived in Hollywood in 1913 to film *The Squaw Man* in a rented barn. The fact that his small company had to share the barn with owner Jacob Stern's horse did not discourage the fledgling filmmaker. He hung a large sign outside that read: JESSE L LASKY FEATURE PLAY COMPANY STUDIO. The film justified De Mille's confidence; it earned almost a quarter of a million dollars and marked the beginning of Hollywood's status as the capital of the young motion picture industry. Although De Mille was not the first filmmaker to work in southern California, the financial success of *The Squaw Man* put the industry's imprimatur on Hollywood and quickened the exodus from New York, which was still dominated by the Motion Picture Patents Trust.

Cecil B De Mille was one of the first movie people to live on a lavish scale. During his early days in Hollywood, he had rented a

Above: Valentino's sudden death in 1926 was the occasion for an unprecedented outpouring of grief on the part of his devoted fans, who erected this touchingly ugly memorial to his memory in Hollywood's de Longpre Park. Actress Patricia Medina was photographed at the site during the filming of Columbia's *Valentino*, released 23 years after the screen idol's death.

Right: Cecil B De Mille, the most influential director in Hollywood history, liked to retire to his 600-acre ranch in Little Tujunga Canyon for weekends in the country.

modest bungalow in Cahuenga Pass for $30 a month. But with the success of such films as *The Virginian* (1914), *The Girl of the Golden West* (1915), and *Male and Female* (1918), which followed *The Squaw Man* in rapid succession during the 1910s, the talented director-producer was soon making $1000 a week. The first of his famous spectacles, *Carmen*, was made in 1915 with opera singer Geraldine Farrar and the popular Wallace Reid. De Mille's profit-sharing plan with Jesse L Lasky generated additional thousands in income. In 1916 the De Milles bought a Spanish-style estate in Hollywood's Laughlin Park. They furnished it comfortably in a mix of Chippendale, Victorian and antique furniture, with Oriental carpets and portieres. Guests were avid for a glimpse of the bathroom because of the director's penchant for scenes of beautiful women taking milk baths in luxurious settings. De Mille recalled in his memoirs the disappointment of two such visitors, who discovered that the director's bathroom 'was just a plain, comfortable, standard American bathroom, without a square inch of onyx or ermine.'

In addition to his understated Laughlin Park residence, De Mille bought a 600-acre ranch in the Sierra Madre near Little Tujunga Canyon. Here he could play the gentleman farmer, growing alfalfa and fruit trees and entertaining actresses on the weekends. He also indulged himself in a gray Locomobile with a red leather interior and a chauffeur-driven limousine. In 1921 De Mille purchased the *Seaward*, a 106-foot yacht with a crew of seven, on which he could entertain eight guests for long cruises. (This was in addition to the 57-foot *Sea Bee*, which made shorter runs to Catalina Island or the Baja California coast.) In his usual leadership role, De Mille was one of the first to take up flying. In 1918 he bought an airplane, in which he took friends aloft over Los Angeles and the Pacific.

Some Hollywood houses passed through many hands during the Glamour Years. The Tudor mansion at 649 West Adams Boulevard in downtown Los Angeles was decorated with tiger skins, crystal balls and mummy cases after Theda Bara bought it during her meteoric career in silent films. But by 1918 audiences were snickering at her vamp routine, and Fox Studios did not renew her contract. Theda (born Theodosia Goodman in Cincinnati) retired into respectability as a housewife, and the house she had owned was purchased by comedy star Roscoe 'Fatty' Arbuckle.

If snooty West Adams Boulevard had been scandalized by Theda Bara, it was outraged by the hard-drinking, party-giving Arbuckle. His career with Mack Sennett had taken him from burlesque and vaudeville to a salary of

$5000 per week as America's favorite slapstick comic. In 1917 he had signed with producer Joe Schenck, who insisted that the hefty actor 'live like a star.' In addition to buying Theda Bara's expensive house, Arbuckle invested $25,000 in a custom-built Pierce Arrow convertible and spent lavishly on entertainment, gifts and jewelry for his wife Minta. But within five years, the death of Virginia Rappe at an all-night drinking party led to the comedian's indictment on first-

Above: De Mille aboard his 106-foot yacht, *Seaward*, with writer Lenore Coffee, left, and his secretary, Gladys Posson.

Below: The De Mille estate in Laughlin Park.

degree murder charges. Despite his acquittal, his career was destroyed. Paramount never released a million dollars' worth of Arbuckle films, and his 1921 contract, which called for him to make three million dollars' worth of shorts over the next three years, was cancelled. He was fortunate to find an occasional directing job under pseudonyms, despite the loyalty of his long-time friend Buster Keaton, who was producing his own films successfully.

The mansion at 649 West Adams Boulevard passed briefly to director Raoul Walsh and his wife, actress Miriam Cooper. When they bought their own place on South Plymouth Boulevard, Arbuckle's former producer, Joe Schenck, bought the property with his wife Norma Talmadge, who had appeared in over 100 films since she began her career at Vitagraph in 1911. (Norma Talmadge kept her jewelry in brown paper bags in the icebox, covered with vegetables.) All three Talmadge sisters were prominent members of the Hollywood scene. Norma's sister Constance, who had also started with Vitagraph, became a popular film comedienne in the 1920s, and Natalie, who acted only occasionally, married Buster Keaton in 1921.

The 'great stone face,' as Keaton was called, found it hard to keep pace with his Brooklyn-born wife's idea of the good life despite his success in films (beginning with *The Butcher Boy* for Fatty Arbuckle in 1917). The newly-wed Keatons first rented a big house on Westchester Place, but Natalie didn't think it was impressive enough for a star who was making over $100,000 a year. She was better pleased with a 20-room mansion on Westmoreland Place, where their neighbors included Mack Sennett, the King of Comedy. Sennett was one of the first to have a screening room in his home, as well as a swimming pool 'about the size of Puget Sound' and two tennis courts.

The years after World War I made Los Angeles and its suburbs a boomtown as the result of increasing movie production, real estate sales and a major jump in oil output – a cornerstone of the local economy for several decades. A consortium of investors including Mack Sennett, Harry Chandler of the *Los Angeles Times* and others spent $20,000 on a

Left: The Beverly Hills Hotel, opened in 1911, attracted new residents into an undeveloped area that had once been primarily bean fields. It would become one of the best-known neighborhoods in the world.

gigantic sign to advertise their 500-acre real-estate tract east of Cahuenga Pass. It read HOLLYWOODLAND in letters 30 feet wide and 50 feet tall, rimmed by light bulbs that made it visible for miles at night. (After World War II 'LAND' was removed by the Hollywood Chamber of Commerce; the huge sign reading HOLLYWOOD remains to this day.) Sennett purchased the adjacent 300-acre mountaintop on which he planned to build a home that would be 'the greatest monument in the world. ... It'll cost two million dollars.' The director planned to defray the cost of the proposed 50-room mansion with its hanging gardens, waterfalls and terraces, by charging admission to the public. But the grandiose scheme never got beyond the architect's renderings. Sennett lost millions in the 1929 stock market crash, and his mountaintop was a casualty of the bankruptcy of Keystone Studios. The $75,000 road that Sennett had constructed to the site of his dream palace ended up leading nowhere.

Meanwhile, Beverly Hills had been developed, in classic Hollywood style, from a gigantic dusty bean field into a fashionable residential community. The bumpy dirt road called Sunset Boulevard, once largely deserted, was by the 1920s the site of imposing mansions and attractively planted cross streets. Crescent, Canyon, Beverly and Rodeo Drives ran north to south between Sunset and Santa Monica Boulevards. The rambling Mission-style Beverly Hills Hotel, built in 1911, became a focal point for the new community, attracting movie people, businessmen and tourists. It served the same purpose as the Hollywood Hotel, four miles to

the east (although Los Angelenos scoffed when it first opened because it was so far out of town).

In 1918 a prospective buyer made the trek into Beverly Hills' Benedict Canyon and climbed the twisting dirt road called Summit Drive to look at a hunting lodge built by a Los Angeles attorney as a weekend retreat. Captivated by the view of Benedict Canyon, sage and wildflowers, and the distant ocean, Douglas Fairbanks paid $35,000 for the 14-acre property. Months later, dozens of workmen were well into the task of total renovation. A second story was added to the lodge, along with another wing, and most of the interior walls were torn down to make more spacious rooms. Architectural plans were entrusted to Max Parker, the art director

Below: Hollywood's king and queen of the 1920s, Douglas Fairbanks Sr and Mary Pickford, relax on a golf outing to Pebble Beach.

128

Right: 'Doug and Mary,' as the press invariably called them, canoeing at Pickfair, the newly renovated hunting lodge that Fairbanks had purchased in 1918 and presented to his wife as a wedding present in 1920.

Below: Theater magnate Sid Grauman, right, directs the casting of the Pickford and Fairbanks footprints in the courtyard of his new Chinese Theatre on Hollywood Boulevard – the beginning of a long tradition.

on many of Fairbanks' films, setting a precedent that would govern Hollywood housing for the next two decades. It was no accident that so many movie stars' homes resembled sets – they were conceived and built by set designers.

At this time, Fairbanks, newly divorced, was seeing Mary Pickford secretly. She was still legally married to her first husband, Owen Moore, although she was separated and living with her mother in a 20-room mansion on Fremont Place. The two had to meet in her studio bungalow, or at the home of Fairbanks' brother Robert, who was his

business manager. So one of his new home's big attractions was its isolation. Another desirable feature was the chance to make over the old hunting lodge in his own image of a country gentleman's estate. Fairbanks wanted something that wouldn't look like the creation of a nouveau riche movie star: it should be comfortable, even luxurious, but not showy or vulgar. These were the guidelines for what would become Pickfair.

When Douglas Fairbanks moved into his new house, the Glamour Years had just begun. In the following decades, Pickfair would see many improvements, especially to the grounds. A 55- by 100-foot swimming pool with a sandy beach along one side was added. A series of ponds for canoeing was dug, and the Beverly Hills Nursery planted hundreds of trees and shrubs on the dry ground that had formerly been covered with chaparral. Fairbanks added a six-stall stable to the outbuildings, and rode regularly on the 14-acre estate or in the nearby Santa Monica Mountains. He hated being alone, so the mock-Tudor-style house was usually full of guests. There were five guest bedrooms on the second floor, plus a bowling alley, billiard room and private screening room. Sometimes the only guest was Mary Pickford. He was eager to marry, but she hung back because of the danger to their careers. The public might not accept her divorce from Moore and remarriage to Fairbanks, popular as they both were. Francis X Bushman's fall from grace as a matinee idol on account of his personal life was a recent sobering example. 'America's Sweetheart' was proud of her success and of

Left: The Fairbankses return from their European honeymoon on 28 July 1920 to a tumultuous public welcome. Douglas Fairbanks Sr thrived on the media attention that followed them everywhere, but his wife would have preferred a more secluded life style.

the millions she had made in pictures. Finally, Fairbanks issued an ultimatum and made his courtship public. Pickford secured her divorce from Moore and the two stars were married in a private double-ring ceremony at the home of a Baptist minister in southern Los Angeles. They returned with the wedding party to Beverly Hills, where Fairbanks declared that his new house was his wedding present to his wife. Two days later, several newspapermen were invited to the house with other guests, and the word was out.

Some early adverse publicity was overcome by the couple's legion of loyal fans, who swamped the Fairbankses when they reached New York in May for a delayed honeymoon in Europe. The crowds were so avid to see them that they could barely get into the Ritz Carlton Hotel, where they were staying. In London, the bride was dragged from an open car and had to be rescued by her husband and four policemen. When they returned to New York, they were greeted by a public delegation headed by Babe Ruth and Jack Dempsey. Soon after returning to California, 'Doug and Mary,' as they were universally known, announced that they would make Doug's Benedict Canyon home their permanent headquarters. It was the press that combined parts of their last names to dub the estate Pickfair – and make it a part of the Hollywood legend.

The nation's most popular couple found that their secluded retreat was not secluded enough to keep them out of the public eye. Newspapers and fan magazines devoted reams of copy to their private life, including who came to dinner and how the living room furniture was arranged. The gregarious Fairbanks enjoyed all the attention, and his wife endured it as the price of stardom. They were photographed on the lawn, in the arbor, out with their dogs and canoeing on one of the ponds. Beginning in 1922, they even worked on the same lot – the 10-acre Pickford-Fairbanks Studio at 7200 Santa Monica Boulevard (later the Goldwyn Studio). But they rarely met at work except for lunch. Dinner was almost always at home – their fans allowed them no peace in nightclubs and restaurants – and guests might include screenwriter Frances Marion, or childhood friend Lillian Gish. Sixteen servants in residence made it easy to invite company on

Below: Pickfair was furnished both tastefully and comfortably and served for years as the focal point of Hollywood social life.

Below: Designer William Cameron Menzies made this sketch for a proposed Fairbanks beach house. The one that was actually built (*right*) was far more modest, but many Hollywood homes did end up looking like movie sets because they were designed by art directors.

the spur of the moment, and the Fairbankses rarely dined alone. When they did dine out at a friend's house, the following notice was sent by their secretary to the prospective hostess:

Mr. and Mrs. Douglas Fairbanks
  beg to inform _____
that it is their desire to be placed
  next to each other at the table.

Those in the know believed that this was evidence of Fairbanks' extreme possessiveness toward 'Little Mary,' rather than of mutual devotion, although their attachment to each other was undeniable. They never spent a night apart during the first eight years of their marriage. However, Fairbanks' jealousy created uncomfortable scenes, as his wife would recall in her autobiography, *Sunshine and Shadow*. 'One day Rudolph Valentino made an unexpected appearance on the Pickfair lawn, which, in the warm months, was our outdoor living room. I never saw Douglas act so fast, and with such painful rudeness, as he did in showing Valentino that he wasn't welcome.'

Invitations to a formal dinner at Pickfair

were eagerly sought, although the food was much more abundant than the wine. Fairbanks had an aversion to liquor because his father had suffered from alcoholism. For years no drinks were served at Pickfair. The highlight of an evening there, in addition to caviar canapés, filet of beef à la Jardinière, and roast wild duck, was a private screening of a new movie and perhaps dancing in the spacious tiled hall adjacent to the living room. Guests who tried to enliven the evening by seduction, as John Barrymore once did in keeping with his reputation as Hollywood's reigning ladies' man, were generally not invited back.

During the mid-1920s, Pickfair was renovated along more elegant lines, as 'the King and Queen of Hollywood' extended their entertaining to visiting nobility: the Duke of York, the King and Queen of Siam, the Crown Prince of Japan and the Duke and Duchess of Alba. A framed picture of Lord and Lady Mountbatten, inscribed 'To Doug and Mary, from Edwina and Dickie,' was displayed prominently. A white grand piano and some nineteenth-century genre paintings were added to the living room, and Fairbanks' bedroom sported a canopied satinwood bed and other delicate furniture that might have seemed more appropriate in his wife's pink-and-green boudouir. The rustic beamed ceiling was pulled out of the dining room, along with the old department-store furniture and Persian carpet, which were relegated to the Fairbanks beach house at Pacific Terrace and Appian Way in Santa Monica. Costly reproductions of eighteenth-century French furniture took their place. Pale green carpeting was laid over the hardwood floor, and built-in china closets with mirrored backs and recessed lighting displayed the couple's collection of porcelain in all four corners of the room.

A footman now stood behind each chair for formal dinners, and weak mixed drinks were allowed for the cocktail hour – no more than two per guest. Wine made its appearance on the dinner table, along with crystal place-card holders and a set of china that had belonged to Napoleon. It was clear that Douglas Fairbanks was beginning to believe his own press. Frances Marion reported that 'He'd kowtow to a duke and a duchess, but when some nice ordinary people were expected, he'd say, "Why are those people coming?" and turn up his nose. But then they'd arrive and he'd swagger up, shoulders back, and put on his act.' Even a good friend like Charlie Chaplin couldn't resist the chance to kid Fairbanks about his royal visitors. One day he sauntered up and said, 'Hello, Doug. How's the duke?' 'What duke?' asked Fairbanks. 'Oh ... any duke,' Chaplin replied. But this penchant for

entertaining the nobility had its drawbacks. The British countess Lady Millicent Haas once came for a weekend and stayed for over a year. One day in 1930, Lillian Gish, then living in New York, got a call from Mary Pickford, who was at a local hotel. 'What in the wide world are you doing here?' asked Gish, who had not expected her friend. Pickford replied, 'Oh, I just couldn't take it any longer, the house, the servants, the company. I'm here in a little hotel room, just for the quiet.'

Pickfair was, in fact, an elaborate menage that was very expensive to operate. Albert, the impeccable major-domo, received a salary of $300 a month for his duties of supervising Fairbanks' extensive wardrobe, organizing parties and overseeing the other help. The cook had a salary of $200 a month and the assistance of a kitchen maid. There were two full-time housemen, a personal maid for Pickford and an upstairs maid for the cleaning. Pickfair's extensive grounds required the care of a head gardener, several day laborers and a watchman, and the garage staff included two chauffeurs.

Fairbanks insisted on paying all these household expenses himself. Other extravagances included his collection of Frederic Remington paintings, a $5000 German shepherd and expensive gifts of clothing and jewelry to friends like Chaplin and Pola Negri. He even planned to charter a steamer for $250,000 and take 50 intimates on a six-month cruise around the world. But this project proved too expensive even for the King of Hollywood. Mary Pickford was more of a realist. She knew how ephemeral popularity could be in the movie business, and most of her substantial earnings were

Above: Adolphe Menjou and his wife in the music room of their home overlooking Santa Monica Canyon in the mid-1920s.

Above: Gloria Swanson's
Beverly Hills home had 22
rooms and 5 baths. She was
23 years old when she bought
the house which was built by
King C Gillette.

invested in real estate and bonds. As a Fairbanks niece once remarked, 'Doug paid the
bills; Mary bought corner lots.'

Beverly Hills soon attracted another silent-
screen star who wanted to live up to her
image. Gloria Swanson, fresh from her
triumphs in such postwar comedies as Cecil B
De Mille's *Don't Change Your Husband*
(1919), bought the three-year-old mansion
that had belonged to King C Gillette, the

Right: Gloria Swanson
returns from Paris with her
new husband, the Marquis de
la Falaise, in 1925, to be feted
by Adolph Zukor, right, and
Jesse L Lasky. Paramount
would offer to raise her salary
to $18,000 per week the
following year.

razor-blade millionaire. It was located at 904
Crescent Drive, above Sunset Boulevard and
opposite the Beverly Hills Hotel. Built in the
Italian Renaissance style, the house was one
of the largest in Beverly Hills – 115 feet wide
and 100 feet deep. It had 22 rooms, 5 baths,
and an automatic elevator, and its thousand-
square-foot terrace overlooked a vast sweep
of lawn studded with palm trees and acacias.
Swanson's goal was to provide herself with a
luxurious setting commensurate with her
success, and she set about turning her new
home into a dream palace that would rival
nearby Pickfair. 'I have decided,' she
announced, 'that while I am a star, I will be
every inch and every moment a star.'

Swanson was only 23 years old when she
bought the Gillette estate, hired four butlers
and gave dinner parties with liveried footmen
behind each guest's chair. Other acquisitions
included three Rolls-Royces, in maroon,
white and black, and a Lancia sports car
upholstered in leopard skin. She installed a
black marble bathroom with a golden tub,
and turned one room into a private movie
theater. The vast reception room was draped
in peacock silk, and the living and dining

rooms boasted elegant furniture, tapestries
and paintings. *Photoplay* raved that 'There is
no star in Hollywood who lives in such gilded
luxury as Gloria Swanson. Gloria's home is
the home of a great lady.'

The exotic-looking Swanson dressed in
keeping with her new setting. The affluent
1920s had rarely seen such an array of fur
coats, evening gowns, headdresses and expensive perfumes as Gloria's $25,000 annual
clothing budget purchased during her heyday. She was often photographed on the
beautiful grounds of her estate with her
Russian wolfhound, Ivan, and her escapades
enlivened many a Hollywood party (including those at Pickfair, which Swanson called
'deadly'). In 1925 Gloria's fans were en-
raptured by her marriage to Henri, Marquis
de la Falaise de la Coudraye, whom she met
while filming *Madame Sans-Gène* on location in France. This was the first marriage
between a screen goddess and a member of
the European nobility, and it set off a wild
celebration in Hollywood. When the new
Marquise returned from Europe with her
husband, schools closed for the day and
thousands of cheering fans packed the streets.

'Welcome Home, Gloria!' proclaimed a great
banner opposite the Paramount studio gate,
where the newlyweds were showered with
rose petals.

The following year, Paramount offered to
raise Swanson's salary to $18,000 per week,
but her popularity was such that she demanded even more, including 50 percent of
the profits of her films. When Paramount
refused, she formed Gloria Swanson, Inc.,
with financial backing from Joseph P
Kennedy, and became a part of United
Artists. This led to friction with resident star
Mary Pickford, whose wholesome image was
very different from that of the sophisticated
Swanson. Years later, the Marquise would
recall an outburst of rivalry over the title role
in *Sadie Thompson* (1928) – that of a prosti-
tute who wants to reform, set in an exotic
South Seas locale. 'Mary'd come over to my
bungalow with her little bee-stung lips and
pout, "I want to do Sadie Thompson." I'm
exactly the same height as she is, maybe just a
half inch taller. But she affected being a child,
with her little Mary Janes and those damned
curls, and I'd wear these enormous high heels
and act like I towered over her. I'd say very

Above: Comedienne Mabel Normand writes a thousand-dollar check for her new Mercer car in the ebullient days before scandal marred her public image.

Right: Thirty-two-year old Wallace Reid in the last photo taken before he entered the sanitarium where he would die at the age of 32. Paramount's most popular male star of the early 1920s had burned himself out through a combination of hyperactivity and drug abuse.

imperiously, "Get out of here, you little shrimp. I'm Sadie Thompson. You can be Sadie Thompson if you let me play Little Annie Rooney – give me your wig!" She'd get furious and say 'These are my own curls!'"

Meanwhile, Beverly Hills had been chosen as home by another popular movie personality: Will Rogers bought an estate at 925 North Beverly Drive and proceeded to give it a Western flavor in keeping with his cowboy image. The rambling Spanish-style house

with its red-tile roof was surrounded by an eight-foot-high brick wall for privacy. Rogers added a swimming pool, stable, riding ring and two log cabins, complete with bunk beds, which the family used as a retreat from unwelcome intruders. Rogers' wife Betty would recall later that 'Formal Christmas Day callers could never find our hideout, concealed by trees and shrubs. We could hear one motorcar after another roll up to our front door and roll away again.'

With four famous movie stars in residence, Beverly Hills was becoming *the* new place to live, in contrast to Hollywood proper or the going-downhill neighborhoods of downtown Los Angeles. The community was still only half developed. Charlie Chaplin reported that around 1920, 'Sidewalks ran along, then disappeared into open fields, and lampposts with white globes adorned empty streets.' At Pickfair, as a houseguest, he would 'listen to the coyotes howling, packs of them invading the garbage cans.' But there was little that the real-estate boom and new money could not accomplish. Many wealthy businessmen, as well as movie stars and studio titans, began building their homes at the terminus of the Pacific Electric train in Beverly Hills. The out-of-town location offered respite from the limelight and a change of scene from grueling days at the studio.

As once-conservative Hollywood became the scene of speakeasies, gambling halls and call girls who claimed to be movie extras, the movie industry, sensitive as it was to public opinion, wanted to dissociate itself from an atmosphere that was becoming increasingly unsavory during Prohibition. Mary Pickford's brother, Jack, was embroiled in a scandal when his wife, former Ziegfeld showgirl Olive Thomas, committed suicide in her Paris hotel room in the throes of heroin addiction. Keystone comedienne Mabel Normand was reputedly addicted to cocaine and involved romantically with Paramount director William Desmond Taylor, who was the victim of an unsolved murder in 1920. When details of his many conquests came out in the press, Sennett withdrew Normand's film *Susanna* (1922) in response to complaints from *Good Housekeeping* magazine. Pretty Mary Miles Minter was another victim of the Taylor scandal. Her passionate love letters to the philandering director, along with more personal effects among his belongings, ended her career with *Drums of Fate* in 1923.

Another scandal that contributed to the exodus from Hollywood was the drug-related death of matinee idol Wallace 'Good Time Wally' Reid in 1923. The handsome six-foot, three-inch leading man had become addicted to morphine; his career as the King of Paramount ended in a sanitarium, where he died at the age of 32. The denouement was an anti-drug film titled *Human Wreckage* (1923), starring Reid's widow, who had been a feature player at Universal under the name Dorothy Davenport. It was billed, with typical filmland understatement, as 'the Greatest Production in the History of Motion Pictures.' Clearly, there was trouble in paradise.

Charlie Chaplin left Hollywood in 1922, to break ground on a big Spanish-style house at 1085 Summit Drive, near Pickfair. His forced marriage to 16-year-old Mildred Harris was almost over. Their child had died in early infancy, and the house they shared briefly on Laughlin Park's De Mille Drive was the scene of increasing estrangement until they separated in 1920. Chaplin did not want an ostentatious home, despite his overwhelming success in films at home and abroad. He was the product of a London slum and had spent most of his childhood in orphanages and workhouses: his priority was comfort and security. The two-story, yellow stucco house on its attractive grounds was decorated to his taste, with a strong leaning toward the appearance of an English gentleman's residence. There were paneled walls, dove-gray color schemes, extensive bookshelves and heavy oak furniture throughout the house. Prints of London under fog and a coal-burning fireplace were additional British touches. The dining-room table was set with fine white Haviland china and a sterling

Above: Lucille Ricksen was featured in the anti-narcotics film *Human Wreckage* (1923), which starred Wallace Reid's widow, Dorothy Davenport; she undertook the project with the covert encouragement of Will Hays.

Left: Charlie Chaplin's estate, nicknamed 'Breakaway House' for the vagaries of its construction. The house stood at 1085 Summit Drive, near Pickfair.

service for 36 imported from Berlin. An incongruous note was struck by cheap domestic glassware instead of the expected crystal. The great comedian's economies often took these eccentric turns. King Vidor complained about the lack of a shower head in the Chaplin bathroom: Charlie was too cheap to pay for a plumber. False economy, in fact, was the hallmark of the house itself; Chaplin had used studio carpenters as much as possible to save money. Unfortunately, they had become so accustomed to designing temporary sets that permanent construction was beyond them. As soon as Chaplin moved in, things began to come apart. Paneling split. Moldings fell. Floors squeaked. Chaplin's friends began calling his new mansion 'Breakaway House,' to the actor's dismay. Nor did the Summit Drive house prove any more auspicious than Laughlin Park to marital happiness. Chaplin's second forced marriage, to child actress Lillita McMurray (Lita Grey), ended up costing him the custody of his two sons and over a million dollars in settlements and lawyers' fees. The scandal that surrounded his wife's complaints against him was extremely damaging to his popularity, although his career, unlike Fatty Arbuckle's, survived the adverse publicity.

Chaplin was a frequent guest at Pickfair, but he did relatively little entertaining at Breakaway House. Errol Flynn played tennis with him quite often during the 1930s, observing later that although Chaplin was

Above: The house of cowboy star Tom Mix was a monument to bad taste, but it suited its free-spending owners, whose Western origins were attested to by innumerable guns, saddles, sombreros and mounted trophies of the hunt.

Right: Vicki Mix favored an opulent look in the master bedroom at 1018 Summit Drive.

'gay, witty and charming,' he was too self-centered to be a good host: 'Unless every bit of conversation centered around him, he was deadly bored.' David Niven complained about the relative scarcity of food and drink at a Chaplin party, remarking that the comedian was 'allergic to laying out large sums of money' on provisions 'to be guzzled by those reckoned to be passengers and noncontributors.'

Another, somewhat dubious, ornament to Summit Drive was Tom Mix's spread at number 1018 – surmounted by the initials *TM* in neon. In fact, the cowboy star's monogram was embossed on every available space like a brand. It appeared on the gates to the driveway, on the front door, over every fireplace in the house. Mix had no inhibitions about letting people know he had made a lot of money in the movies. Always extravagant, often vulgar, he made his house a monument to his career. When his favorite horse, Tony, died, its tail was turned into a bellpull. In the dining room was an illuminated fountain where streams of colored water played.

The cowboy star's fourth wife, Vicki Mix, a former cowgirl, and sometime actress, had her own ideas of elegance. In her private parlor on one side of the entrance hall, and in the master bedroom, ersatz Louis XVI furniture swathed in ornate drapery contrasted with her husband's silver-embossed saddles, rifles and pistols. It was a long way from riding the range in pursuit of stray steers. Mrs Mix also had the largest jewelry collection in the Hollywood of the 1920s, where her husband was making $17,000 a week. Diamonds and sapphires were her favorite

jewels, and she wore them to breakfast. Not to be outshone, Tom Mix appeared at Hollywood galas in a purple tuxedo with matching boots and Stetson, glittering with diamond stickpins, rings and other jewelry including diamond-and-platinum belt buckles. Anita Loos recalls that Tom Mix was 'just an ordinary cowboy with a cowboy's mentality,' but he certainly had a good time spending almost everything he earned in the mid-1920s. His off-screen antics were very much at variance with his wholesome, tee-totaling screen image. On one occasion, he got into a drunken brawl with fellow cowboy actor Art Accord, then rode Tony up the main stairs to the second floor in a blaze of gunfire (directed at the ceiling) to the accompaniment of wild yells in the best frontier tradition.

Tom Mix's flamboyant residence was by no means unusual in Glamour Years Hollywood. The only architectural style indigenous to Southern California was the well-worn Spanish hacienda. Newly rich movie stars and oil tycoons wanted something different, preferably romantic, and an amazing array of building styles mushroomed all over the Los Angeles area. There were pseudo-Tudor residences shaded by incongruous palm trees, 'Olde English' cottages straight from a children's storybook, would-be French chateaux, miniature Arabian mosques and pseudo-Indian dwellings in the pueblo style. Architect Frank Lloyd Wright, who came west to design the contemporary Hollyhock House for heiress Aline Barnsdall, stayed to build three other houses in the Hollywood Hills. All were in

Hollywood architecture during the Glamour Years was exactly what one would expect from the fantasy capital of the world – fantastic. *At left*, the one-of-a-kind Sphinx Realty office. *Bottom left*, a Tail of the Pup hot-dog stand – form follows function. *Below*, the Zep Diner, modeled on the airborne zeppelin. *Right*, the Crossroads of the World, at Sunset Boulevard near Highland.

Bottom right: Grauman's Chinese Theatre, showing *Hell's Angels* in 1930. *Bottom far right*, the startling apparition of the Chili Dog Cafe.

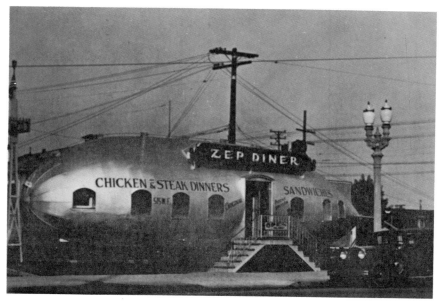

Right: The massive sets for the Babylonian sequence of D W Griffith's *Intolerance* (1916) at Sunset and Hillhurst in East Hollywood rise behind typical southern Californian bungalows. It was several years before they were dismantled.

Far right: The storybook Willat Studio, a replica of Hansel and Gretel's cottage, was originally located at 6509 Washington Boulevard in Culver City. In the foreground of this 1921 photograph are Irvin Willat and Barbara Bedford.

Below: The Arabian-nights sets for *The Thief of Bagdad* dominate the Pickford-Fairbanks Studio lot in 1923, as US Navy visitors come to marvel.

Right: No one who visited John Barrymore's Tower Road estate could doubt that the great actor (right) was an animal lover. In addition to his stuffed specimens, Barrymore had an extensive private zoo, including an aviary for 300 different kinds of birds.

the concrete-block, neo-Mayan style, and the largest of the three, the Ennis house on Vermont Avenue, looked like an ancient monument suitable for human sacrifice. However, Wright was extremely critical of prevailing Southern California architectural styles, which he called 'the eclectic procession to and fro in the rag-tag and cast-off of the ages.'

Another arresting feature of the landscape was 'programmatic architecture' of commercial buildings, by which form signified function. Hollywood abounded in 10-foot-tall oranges that dispensed juice, giant doughnuts, and mammoth hot dogs encased in buns, like the Tail of the Pup. The most familiar example of this trend was the first Brown Derby restaurant, with its invitation to 'Eat in the Hat' displayed outside.

Bizarre mixtures of styles were a commonplace; stars like John Barrymore imported ancient Scottish fireplaces and Italian stained-glass windows for installation in their Spanish-style mansions. Flamboyant personalities like Pola Negri lived in conservative copies of Mount Vernon. Director George Fitzmaurice started building a traditional Spanish hacienda, only to have it pooh-poohed by his fiancée, actress Florence Vidor, who wanted something along Tudor lines. While Fitzmaurice was changing gears on the construction, his intended decided to marry violinist Jascha Heifetz instead, leaving the jilted director with a very strange hybrid of a house.

The movie industry contributed its share of exotica in the form of leftover sets that sometimes stood for years. The minarets and domes from the Douglas Fairbanks adventure film *The Thief of Bagdad* (1924) gave Culver City a Middle Eastern air. Elaborate Babylonian stage sets for D W Griffith's expensive failure *Intolerance* (1916) dwarfed the bungalows of suburban Los Angeles for several years after the picture came out in 1916. Hollywood movie palaces set the tone for the nation during the 1920s: the Spanish baroque Million Dollar Theater and Grauman's famous Chinese and Egyptian Theaters were widely copied. Even the movie studio buildings resembled stage sets. Charlie Chaplin's La Brea Avenue studio featured a street full of mock-Tudor cottages. B-picture producer Irvin Willat went even farther: his studio was a replica of Hansel and Gretel's cottage fronting a rock-bordered artificial pond. The building was designed to look old and weathered, with mismatched shingles on the roof and shutters hanging askew.

By 1927 some 60,000,000 Americans were going to the movies every week. Studio chiefs were telling their stars where to live, what to wear and what kind of car to drive to maintain the right image with their legions of fans. A hot-dog vendor set up his stand outside the gates of Pickfair, and entrepreneurs went into business as guides to movie stars' homes. It was becoming increasingly difficult for movie people – even the richest – to find suitable houses, as realtors doubled their prices as soon as they heard a star was interested. Some, like John Barrymore, who bought King Vidor's Tower Road home, got friends and relatives to act as their front men in negotiating a purchase. Barrymore paid a relatively modest $50,000 for the Spanish-style house he called Belle Vista, but that was his

only economy. As soon as he took title to the property, he bought four acres next door for a total of seven acres. Over the next 10 years, the original five-room house grew to 16 separate buildings (including the Marriage House that he built after he married Dolores Costello). As their children were born, he added another wing to the new house. He also built a tower above his bedroom accessible only by a trap door – here he could be alone, once he pulled his ladder up after him. Barrymore called it 'my blessed hideaway from the world of idiocy.'

Barrymore spent a great deal of money on landscaping Belle Vista with the help of his gifted Japanese gardener, Nishimura, and numerous assistants. In addition to rare and expensive plantings, the grounds contained a bowling green, a skeet range, fountains and fish ponds, an artificial waterfall and six pools. Equally expensive was his collection of animals, including 300 different birds for whom he built a large aviary that simulated a natural habitat. Carnivorous and herbiverous species were separated by a partition, and the eminent actor spent hours watching his birds from a nearby granite bench. When Belle Vista's zoo keeper ran out of rotten meat for Barrymore's prized vulture, Maloney, 'the great profile' was not above foraging in nearby garbage cans to feed the bird.

Besides the aviary, Barrymore's private zoo included opossums, kinkajous, mouse deer, dozens of Siamese cats and 19 dogs, including 11 greyhounds and several Saint Bernards. All of the estate's buildings were tastefully and elegantly furnished with good antiques, marble mantlepieces and Oriental rugs. Diana Barrymore described the effect as that of 'a little village, a hacienda of buildings with red tiled roofs, iron grilled windows and gardens.'

But even Belle Vista was eclipsed by the 22-acre estate of comedian Harold Lloyd, whose centerpiece was a 40-room mansion. Greenacres had 12 different formal gardens, a nine-hole golf course and an 800-foot-long canoe pond. Here Lloyd spent over $2,000,000 of the fortune he made playing a bespectacled, bumbling and sympathetic adolescent in such popular films as *Safety Last* (1923) and *Girl Shy* (1924). Five years after Lloyd married his leading lady Mildred Davis, the couple moved from their Irving Boulevard home in downtown Los Angeles to Beverly Hills' most impressive estate at 1225 Benedict Canyon Drive. The 1929 housewarming was a four-day affair with a specially constructed dance floor on the lawn and continuous band music. (The Lloyds were still finding left-over guests around days after the party.)

Visitors approached the 36,000-square-foot house by way of a long palm-lined driveway that took them past the seven-car garage, servants' quarters and greenhouses into the main courtyard of the pink Spanish-style mansion, which had 26 bathrooms in addition to its 40 rooms. Lloyd furnished the house entirely to his own specifications, including the rugs and drapery. The sunken living room had a gold-leaf coffered ceiling, a stone fireplace and a forty-rank pipe organ of the type used in movie palaces of the time. The dining room could seat two dozen guests and the private theater, a hundred. Thirty-two servants were hired to keep the estate running smoothly.

The three Lloyd children had a four-room playhouse in one of the gardens, complete with thatched roof, plumbing, electricity and miniature furniture. There was an Olympic-size pool, facilities for handball and tennis, 12 fountains and a 120-foot waterfall that descended a steep hillside from the terrace into the canoe lake. Jack Warner had his own nine-hole golf course next door, and occasionally he and Lloyd would put a walkway over the fence so that their guests could play all 18 holes. However, even the Lloyds sometimes found Greenacres overwhelming. Mildred Lloyd once confided to Hedda Hopper that they had spent an hour riding up and down in one of the mansion's two elevators on the day they moved in. 'It was,' she recalled 'the only cozy place in the house.'

In addition to their main houses, many movie-colony members built beach houses in Santa Monica: during the 1920s and '30s, they stretched for a mile along the ocean. Many of these retreats began as cottages, but they soon grew into seaside mansions, of which Louis B Mayer's was one of the most impressive. MGM art director Cedric Gibbons had designed it in the popular Spanish style, with foot-thick walls for insulation against the heat. The house had 20 rooms and 13 bathrooms done in onyx and marble, and the Beverly Hills Nursery kept replanting the grounds with flowers and shrubs that were ready to bloom – Mrs Mayer didn't want to wait years for an attractive garden.

Douglas Fairbanks and Mary Pickford had a surprisingly modest beach house, which they furnished with castoffs from Pickfair. Other part-time residents of Santa Monica included Joe Schenck and Norma Talmadge, Mae West, Sam Goldwyn, Ben Lyon and Bebe Daniels, Jesse Lasky, Cary Grant and

Above: John Barrymore's beautiful two-masted schooner *Mariner* competed in the Los Angeles-Honolulu race for the Lipton Trophy.

Harold Lloyd. Even Will Rogers took time from his beloved ranch in Pacific Palisades to stay at the shore.

The real showplace in Santa Monica, however, was the dream palace built for Marion Davies by William Randolph Hearst – an 80-room compound with 55 baths that could accommodate up to 2000 guests for a party. It was estimated that Hearst spent several million dollars on the original building and furnishings and twice that in ongoing renovations and running expenses over a 15-year period. The place was so big that tourists assumed it was a resort hotel and frequently stopped at the guardhouse to ask about rooms.

The neo-colonial main house included a lavish Gold Room for entertaining, a cavernous dining room, a ballroom and a private theater. In the basement was a 'tavern' that sat 50 guests: it had been imported from England where it was originally an Elizabethan public house. The huge swimming pool was crossed by a Venetian-style bridge of marble.

Hearst had been determined to make Marion Davies a star since he fell in love with her when she was a chorine in Florenz Ziegfeld's *Follies of 1917*. The newspaper magnate was then 54 years old, and Davies was 20. Two years after their romance began, he formed Cosmopolitan Pictures (which later became part of MGM) to make Marion's films, spending lavishly on top directors, public-relations people and dramatic coaches. Marion (whom he called 'Muggins') had a natural flair for comedy, but Hearst insisted on starring her in showy and romantic costume epics, in which she did not appear to advantage, since she was not a skilled dramatic actress. And the publicity power he wielded through his publishing empire resulted in overkill: Charlie Chaplin complained that 'One could not open a Hearst magazine or newspaper without a large picture of Marion. All this only kept the public away from the box office.' It was estimated that Hearst lost $7,000,000 on Marion's career.

Hearst and Marion were deeply in love until his death, and he wanted to marry the attractive and vivacious young actress, but his wife Millicent refused to divorce him. Shunned by some members of the Hollywood social set, Marion compensated for her ostracism as a 'kept woman' by giving lavish and expensive parties at her beach house, her Beverly Hills mansion, or the fabled 250,000-acre San Simeon ranch, in San Luis Obispo County. (Anita Loos met an Indian guide at San Simeon who had never left the property since his birth 70 years before.)

San Simeon was a monument to Hearst's incredible wealth and to his passion for collecting antiques and *objets d'art* from all over the world. In partnership with architect Julia Morgan, he created a fantastic world of his own on a hilltop overlooking the central California coast – *La Cuesta Encantada*, or The Enchanted Hill. The beautiful Spanish-style complex was almost 30 years in the building, and even then it was never finished. The first of three main houses, Casa del Monte, was livable by the early 1920s. By 1924 the other two – Casa del Mar and Casa del Sol – were ready for use, although they were constantly enlarged in the form of additional guest suites well into the 1930s. Hearst and his agents ransacked Europe for treasures with which to embellish what came to be known as 'Hearst Castle' (now the Hearst Monument). The main building's Assembly Room contained the Great Barney Mantel, Flemish tapestries, Italian Renaissance choir stalls, marble statuary and ornate silver candlesticks. Hearst's Gothic study was a peerless example of the style. The indoor

Left: The exquisite facade of the Great House at San Simeon, wreathed in exotic plantings and pediments. Architect Julia Morgan spent years designing with Hearst the incredible complex that he called The Enchanted Hill.

Below: The baronial refectory at San Simeon, flanked by monks' stalls and massive candelabra. Overhead are ducal banners from Venice, Siena and Florence.

Right: Hearst's northern California estate, Wyntoon, which he used mainly for summer vacations by the mid-1930s, preferring to spend most of the year at San Simeon.

Below: Hearst entertains dinner guests in his great dining hall, which originated in a Spanish monastery. Marion Davies, in polka-dot dress, is seated back to camera.

Roman Pool was beautifully tiled in green, gold and blue, and two rooftop tennis courts were the setting for San Simeon's most popular outdoor recreation. The acquisition of an ancient temple fragment inspired construction of the magnificent Neptune Pool, a colonnaded basin dominated by the temple facade.

On the grounds, spreading California live oaks were the hilltop's main ornament until English gardener Nigel Keep was hired to develop extensive orchards and exquisite flower gardens. A pergola was built west of the main grounds. In 1924 the acquisition of 40 Montana buffalo marked the beginning of San Simeon's free-range zoo (guests were warned by signs along the driveway that 'Animals have right of way'). It became the world's largest private zoo, with a collection that included zebras, ostriches and water buffalo. (David Niven recalled that Hearst's love of animals was so great that he left tidbits of food around for the mice in La Casa Grande's dining hall – until they multiplied so rapidly that he agreed reluctantly to have them trapped, provided they were not hurt in the process. Once released, the delighted mice headed straight back to the kitchen.)

By 1935 San Simeon had become Hearst's favorite and primary residence, although he still spent summers at his northern California estate, Wyntoon. Where San Simeon was magnificent. Wyntoon was a page from a children's storybook, with its steep, gabled roofs and Bavarian facade surrounded by towering evergreens. The names of the buildings reflected the element of make-believe: Angel House, Cinderella House, Brown Bear and the Pinnacles. But it was at San Simeon that Hearst and Marion Davies entertained Hollywood – increasingly so in the early 1930s, as Pickfair's prestige began to dwindle along with its owners' careers. Hearst biographer W A Swanberg alleged that 'Hollywood was divided into two castes: people who had been guests at San Simeon and those who had not.'

The castle's guest books were a *Who's Who* of Hollywood's Glamour Years. Their signators included Louis B Mayer, Greta Garbo, John Gilbert, Norma Shearer, Irving Thalberg, David Niven and hundreds of

Left: C Aubrey Smith, seated right, headed up the Hollywood Cricket Club in the mid-1930s. Other members included, front row, from left, Bob Finlayson, Murray Kinnell, Robert Montgomery and Stanley Mann. David Niven stands behind Smith, flanked by George Allen and Nigel Bruce.

others. Liquor did not flow freely at San Simeon, because Hearst was concerned about Marion's drinking, which became increasingly problematic, but enterprising guests smuggled in their own supplies. Costume parties were a favorite entertainment at all the Hearst houses. Themes included the Circus (2000 people attended the party), Early America, a Midsummer Night's Dream, the Wild West and Babies, at which the stars showed up in knee pants, Mary Janes and oversized hair bows. Several hundred rented costumes were kept at the beach house for guests who didn't have time to find the appropriate outfit.

Marion Davies was extremely generous with both money and clothes, lending freely from her lavish wardrobe. She liked to joke that in her house, the first one up was the best dressed. For all her wealth, she was a warm and generous person, devoted to Hearst. When he came upon financial hard times in the late 1930s as a result of incredible spending, she sold her jewelry and pooled her savings and real-estate investments to stave off his bankruptcy.

Anita Loos observed that: 'More money was squandered on Marion than on all the gold diggers of the fabulous Twenties. But she never had to dig. She was merely a placid target toward which riches zoomed like steel to a magnet. As a fledgling New York chorus girl, she'd been the sweetheart of another wealthy publisher, the owner of the *Brooklyn Eagle*. By the time she met Hearst, Marion had grown so used to money that it never entered her calculations.'

In the early 1930s, fashionable Summit Drive got a new resident in the person of Ronald Colman, the leader of Hollywood's British contingent. Colman added to the English ambience of his ivy-covered Tudor-style house by replacing the native bougainvilleas and oleanders with clipped yew hedges. Hollywood was going through a

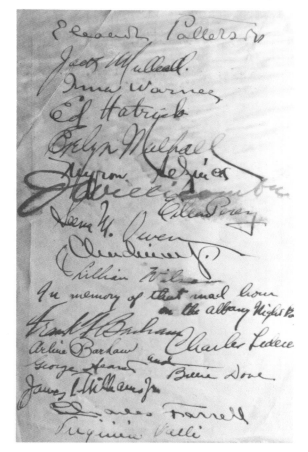

Left: A page from one of San Simeon's guest books. It was said that Hollywood was divided into two castes: people who had been guests at San Simeon and those who had not.

Above: The gracious Spanish-mission style Bel Air Hotel.

Below: Carole Lombard and Clark Gable at their ranch at Encino.

British period at this time: there were 22 cricket clubs in California when David Niven arrived in 1934. C Aubrey Smith was captain of the Hollywood Cricket Club, which Niven joined. In his autobiography *The Moon's a Balloon*, the British actor reported that 'Crashes were frequent on Sunset Boulevard on Sunday afternoons, when amazed local drivers became distracted by the

sight of white flannel trousers and blazers on the football ground of U.C.L.A.' Other members of the British colony were Nigel and Bunnie Bruce, Ernest and Elsie Torrance, E E Clive, Eric Blore and Basil Rathbone. They were in demand for such pictures as *Mutiny on the Bounty* (1935), *David Copperfield* (1936), *National Velvet* (1944), *Lives of a Bengal Lancer* (1935) and the various Sherlock Holmes films.

In 1932 Sam and Frances Goldwyn moved from Hollywood Boulevard to a gracious Colonial house at 1200 Laurel Lane in Beverly Hills. The six-thousand-square-foot house was furnished with attractive antiques and Goldwyn's collection of paintings, including the works of Renoir, Picasso and Matisse. Frances Goldwyn had included in the plans a wood-paneled den that doubled as a screening room, and the great Goldwyn proclaimed himself satisfied – he had left the whole construction project to his wife.

By the late 1930s, many movie people were relocating to the exclusive development of Bel Air, in the hills above Sunset Boulevard. During the 1920s they had been barred from the expensive neighborhood developed by oil millionaire Alfonzo Bell, but the financial distress of the Depression Years made them welcome. The community offered polo fields, tennis courts and an 18-hole golf course that became the Bel Air Country Club. And there

were 65 miles of bridle paths in the hills sur-rounding the Bel Air Stables on Stone Canyon Road. Actress Colleen Moore bought a large estate on St Pierre Road, and in 1935 Warner Baxter built a stone mansion in the Gothic style on a five-acre Nimes Road property. In 1940 17-year-old Judy Garland, who had recently completed *The Wizard of Oz*, had a 10-room house built for herself and her mother at 1231 Stone Canyon Road. It had tennis and badminton courts, pinball machines and a secret hideaway concealed behind a built-in bookcase.

The growing trend toward simplicity that came with the Depression years was exempli-fied by the San Fernando Valley home of Clark Gable and Carole Lombard. It was a 30-acre working ranch, surrounded by citrus groves, and the main house was a relatively modest white-brick and frame affair fur-nished in Early American style. The fact that there were no guest bedrooms indicated that the Gables sought privacy in their rural setting – complete with horses, cows and pigsty (which had, however, no pigs). 'The King' was often photographed milking cows or mending fences to show that success hadn't gone to his head. Though most of these pictures were staged by publicists. Gable was, in fact, a real outdoorsman who welcomed a chance to get out of the limelight. He was almost universally well liked and well spoken of in a professional environment that was more conducive to jealousy and scandal than to mutual esteem. He and Carole Lombard had an unusually close relationship and Gable was devastated by her death in a plane crash during a War Bond drive in 1942.

By the time the Glamour Years ended, the dream-palace era was over too. Depression, divorce, career fluctuations and changing tastes all contributed to the demise of the notion that 'a star must live like a star.'

Celebrities of the new era like Katharine Hepburn, William Powell and Cary Grant did not build extravagant stage sets for their off-screen lives. Their image was more re-laxed than that of the hectic early years. Or perhaps they had come full circle to the view expressed by D W Griffith, who had said to director Rex Ingram in the pioneer days of filmmaking: 'We are building on sand, Rex, just building on sand.'

PACESETTERS
AND MAVERICKS

With or without the help of its publicity machine, Glamour Years Hollywood spawned some of the most colorful, talented, grandiose, exotic and off-beat personalities in the history of American entertainment. They are impossible to pigeonhole in any one category, since they reflected the changing tastes and dreams of the American public over several turbulent decades of national and cinema history.

In 1919 the screen was still dominated by stars who reflected the old-fashioned American values of hard work, sacrifice, marital fidelity and the triumph of innocence over experience. The essential romanticism of D W Griffith imbued the careers of the female stars whom the path-breaking filmmaker had introduced to a national audience: Mary Pickford, Dorothy and Lillian Gish, Mae Marsh, and Blanche Sweet and Bessie Love, whose names even reflected the type of characters they portrayed.

Mary Pickford (born Gladys Smith), 'America's Sweetheart,' was actually Canadian by birth. She became a child actress and her family's principal support after her father died when she was five years old. In 1907 she was taken up by Broadway showman David Belasco, who changed her name and brought her to New York. From 1909, still in her teens, Pickford worked for Griffith's Biograph Company, where her delicate, childlike beauty and well-developed acting skills brought her increasing popularity in such roles as *Tess of the Storm Country* (1914), *Cinderella* (1914), *Rags* (1915) and *Rebecca of Sunnybrook Farm* (1917).

Her first release after World War I was *Daddy Long Longs* (1919) distributed by First National. By this time Pickford had joined several different companies in her search for better salaries and more independence. After this, all her films were released through United Artists, of which she was a co-founder in 1919.

Pickford's desire to take on more mature and demanding roles like those she portrayed in *Rosita* (1923) or *Dorothy Vernon of Haddon Hall* (1924) was resisted to the end by the public, which preferred her as *Pollyanna* (1919) and *Little Annie Rooney* (1925). When sound came in, by which time she was in her thirties, Pickford was at a turning point in her career. Although she made four talking pictures that proved she had the artistic capability to make the transition to the sound medium, she chose to retire before her legend could be compromised by repudiation of the character type that the public had foisted upon her – that of a childlike Victorian heroine unsuited to the Jazz Age.

At the height of her career, the first movie star had received 18,000 letters a week, which she answered with the help of 18 secretaries. Pickford recalled for Walter Wagner that 'Hollywood was such a lovely place then. Everybody knew everybody, and it seemed to me that it was such a small place. It was so intimate. We had the Mayfair Club, what they called the Hollywood Four Hundred, and we'd meet once a month at the Biltmore Hotel for dinner and dancing. Everyone was there, Valentino, Chaplin ... In those days we were all one big happy family.'

Pickford's friend Lillian Gish was instrumental in preventing her from destroying her old films after she retired. The two had come to Hollywood with Biograph in the mid-1910s and remained lifelong friends. Lillian Gish was an actress of rare vibrancy and creativity, whose unusual beauty was well suited to the romantic roles Griffith devised for her in such films as *Broken Blossoms* (1919) and *Way Down East* (1920). Her riveting performances lifted melodrama into the realm of art. Gish brought her own innovative approach to acting, which she described in a *Sight and Sound* interview with cinema

Previous pages: A 1930s publicity still inscribed 'Greetings from Clark Gable, Metro-Goldwyn-Mayer featured player' – soon to be known as 'the King.'

Below: King Vidor, center, flanked by cameraman Henrik Sartov and producer Irving Thalberg, directs Lillian Gish in her first picture for MGM, *La Bohème* (1926).

Top left: Doug and Mary peek through the portholes of SS *Leviathan* upon their return from a triumphal tour of Europe in 1924.

Above: The famous Gish death scene in *La Bohème*, which frightened everyone on the set into believing that the great actress had actually died before the cameras. Her costar is John Gilbert.

Left: Mary Pickford's public was unwilling to let her grow up. She was still playing child and adolescent roles well into her twenties.

Above: Lillian Gish arrives home from a long day of shooting in 1921. She and her sister Dorothy lived with their mother in modest rented quarters for several years after they arrived in Hollywood.

historian David Robinson, citing the famous closet scene in *Broken Blossoms*: 'You know the scene in the closet, where I spin round and round in terror as Donald Crisp is trying to open the door to beat me and kill me. I worked that out myself, and never told Griffith what I was going to do. You see, if I had told him, he'd have made me rehearse it over and over again, and that would have

Right: Angelic-looking Bessie Love takes to the jungle for her role in First National's *The Lost World* (1925).

spoilt it. It had to be spontaneous, the hysterical terror of a child. Well, when I came to play the scene in front of the camera, I did it as I'd planned – spinning and screaming terribly (I was a good screamer; Mr. Griffith used to encourage me to scream at the top of my voice). When we finished, Mr. Griffith was very pale.'

Many similar accounts of Lillian Gish's intensity before the camera are part of film history: her baptism of the dying child in *Way Down East* was 'so real and affecting that the child's real, off-screen father fainted.' And King Vidor, who directed her in *La Bohème* (1926), was convinced - with everyone else on the set – that she had died when they shot the death scene.

Bessie Love first appeared in Griffith's *Intolerance* (1916) to critical acclaim, despite the film's failure at the box office. Her playful good humor came across on screen and was an asset when she co-starred with the high-spirited young Douglas Fairbanks Sr after Griffith formed the Triangle Company.

Love's training with Griffith carried her on to a career as a dramatic actress in the mid-1920s and helped her make a successful transition to talking pictures, in which she achieved success as one of the first film-musical stars. Other sentimental heroines in the prewar mode were not so fortunate: Mae Marsh, for example, was badly cast in the 1920s and ended by playing character roles to the end of her life. Blanche Sweet made a successful comeback in the 1920s after a period away from the screen.

Mabel Normand was one of Hollywood's most irrespressible characters, both on and off-screen, during the early Glamour Years. She started as an artist's model and then got work as an extra with Biograph. Mack Sennett's gift for direction actualized her comic potential, although their stormy personal relationship often hindered their work. Sennett showcased the gifted comedienne in the feature *Mickey* (1918), and she made numerous shorts with Arbuckle and Chaplin. Eddie Le Veque, 'the last of the Keystone Kops,' recalled that 'In its heyday the Keystone lot was called the Crazy Factory. Some actors thought it beneath their dignity to work slapstick for Sennett,' but 'The Keystone Kops pictures had a sparkle to them, a spontaneity that pictures today seem to lack.' Normand was credited with inventing the pie-throwing squence that became such a fixture in slapstick comedy, and her fabulous wardrobe and well-publicized pranks kept her in the limelight until ill health and scandal, plus a final rift with Sennett, sent her into retirement.

Pearl White, the athletic all-American heroine of countless serials, had a major

America and its simple virtues and values. Ray came to the Ince company from the theater to make popular films like *An Old-Fashioned Boy* (1920) and *The Old Swimmin' Hole* (1921) However, his popularity waned after Ince's death. Barthelmess enjoyed a longer career, beginning with his Griffith roles in *Broken Blossoms* (1919), *Way Down East* (1920) and *The Idol Dancer* (1920). He had enormous success in King's *Tol'able David* (1921), but struggled thereafter against type-casting as the grassroots American boy.

William S Hart was the greatest of the early Western stars: he came to Hollywood from a career on the stage with Helen Modjeska and David Belasco, which included Western roles. His first major success was *The Squaw Man* (1919) for Cecil B De Mille, followed closely by *The Virginian* (1919). His angular face and serious mien suited him ideally to the role of nature's nobleman, and his popularity con-

Left: 'Can't keep him down,' complains Mary Pickford to the press, as her husband launches into one of his acrobatic stunts for the camera.

Below: Mabel Normand was as well known for her real-life clowning as for her screen antics in Mack Sennett's Keystone Comedies.

following during the early Glamour Years. She tangled successfully with rustlers, bandits, gamblers, seducers and other ne'er-do-wells week in and week out, setting the style for action-oriented heroines of both the serial and Western genres.

Douglas Fairbanks Sr, unlike many Hollywood pioneers, came from a prosperous middle-class background that proved too confining for his native energy and high spirits. He tried a variety of careers before he turned to the Broadway stage and then signed with Triangle. A series of light comedies established him as the epitome of the All-American boy – an athletic optimist who was quick to puncture the pretensions of stuffy Easterners and the fads of the day. A hero in the Theodore Roosevelt mold of strenuous outdoor activity, Fairbanks made over two dozen popular films after his initial success in *His Picture in the Papers* (1915). As a co-founder of United Artists, in the early 1920s he turned to a series of costume spectacles that were equally successful with his public: *The Mark of Zorro* (1920), *The Three Musketeers* (1921), *Robin Hood* (1922), *The Thief of Baghdad* (1924), *Don Q, Son of Zorro* (1925). In these and other productions, he not only acted, but supervised every aspect of production, including occasional direction and script-writing. His marriage and professional relationship with Mary Pickford enhanced both their careers, although the couple as divorcées had originally feared to marry. As it turned out, 'Doug and Mary' were even more popular with their fans as a couple than either had been alone.

Silent stars Charles Ray and Richard Barthelmess carried on the Griffith tradition in their early roles, which glorified rural

156

tinued through the release of his last picture, King Baggott's *Tumbleweeds* (1925). Hart's old-fashioned morality and humorlessness perhaps seem a little dated today, but he conveyed a feeling of respect and attachment for the land and a vanishing way of life that struck a sympathetic chord with American audiences.

Other cowboy stars, many of them real cowboys and graduates of the old Wild West shows, enjoyed great popularity with movie goers of the 1920s. They lacked Hart's stature, but their energetic, often humorous, portrayals were in demand. Harry Carey made numerous Westerns for John Ford, as did George O'Brien, whose sensitive acting contributed so much to *The Iron Horse* (1924) and *Three Bad Men* (1926). Tim McCoy, Ken Maynard, Hoot Gibson and William Russell all had their followings.

Meanwhile, a new type of film pioneered by Cecil B De Mille, Ernst Lubitsch and their followers was bringing more sophisticated characters to the screen in comedies that had no place for the old-fashioned virtues and heroes. Adolphe Menjou was pre-eminent among the male stars of this genre. His worldly-wise performance in *A Woman of Paris* (1923) brought roles in *Broadway After Dark* (1924), *The Marriage Circle* (1924), *The Grand Duchess and the Waiter* (1926), *Are Parents People* (1926) and at least three dozen other sophisticated comedies. Menjou was one of the fortunate silent-film stars whose career was only enhanced by the advent of talking pictures; he continued acting into his old age.

Wallace Reid – handsome, well-educated, sophisticated – was a popular matinee idol in such films as De Mille's *The Affairs of Anatol* (1921), for Paramount. His addiction to drugs was rumored around Hollywood before the public suspected anything about it, and the studio reportedly sent him to a remote mountain cabin with orders to get off drugs

Below: Debonair Adolphe Menjou, 'the best liked of the movie villains,' smiles for his public en route from Hollywood to New York to film a new thriller in 1925.

and alcohol – to no avail. Jimmy Fidler, then a Paramount publicist, claimed that Reid was 'a nice guy who couldn't say no to an invitation, to do anything. He played scores of benefits … He was on the go so many hours that he broke his health down, and in order to keep going and do his job well in pictures, he went the Judy Garland routine, pills to keep him up and then on to stronger stuff.' His death was a shattering blow to his fans, as was the death of Rudolph Valentino, also in his early thirties.

Valentino, uniquely photogenic, had brought a new kind of brooding sensuality to the screen. As *Life* would sum it up in an article of 15 January 1950, he symbolized for the newly emancipated female fan 'everything wild and wonderful and illicit in nature.' His flawless skin; dark, melancholy eyes under expressive brows; and patent-leather hair were a radical departure from the image of the conventional American hero.

Italian by birth, Rodolpho Pietro Filiberto Guglielmi had failed his course at the Venice Military Academy and emigrated to America, where he supported himself variously as a gardener, a waiter and an exhibition dancer. Small parts as an Italian villain led to his discovery by June Mathis, who cast him in Rex Ingram's *Four Horsemen of the Apocalypse* (1921). Ingram's directorial genius made the most of Valentino's natural grace, intensity and eroticism. His success with the public was immediate, and Clarence Brown's *The Eagle* (1925) confirmed his popularity. Today Valentino is remembered mainly for his

Above: Rudolph Valentino set a new standard for masculine desirability with his chiseled features, natural grace and brooding sensuality. Rex Ingram was the first director to maximize his undeniably limited acting skills, in *Four Horsemen of the Apocalypse* (1921), the beginning of his brief but meteoric career.

Far left: Wallace Reid with his infant son in 1919, when the handsome actor was 28 years old.

Left: Homely William S Hart subdued a lot of wild horses on the Hollywood frontier.

exotic desert-song pictures like *The Sheik* (1921) and *Son of the Sheik* (1926) – his last picture before his death of peritonitis at the age of 31. His brief career suffered from his personal extravagance, difficulties with his producers, many caused by the interference of his ambitious wife, Natacha Rambova, and bad publicity about his degenerating influence upon American manhood. But the public outpouring of grief at his death, including the suicides of distraught female fans, was unprecedented and became at once a part of the Hollywood legend.

Female stars who specialized in the newly popular woman-of-the-world roles in the early 1920s comedies included Clara Kimball Young, who was managed by Myron Selznick during the most successful part of her career. The versatile Anna Q Nilsson was a beautiful Swedish actress who was equally at home in Westerns, comedies and dramas. Alice Terry, who worked with Rex Ingram in his romantic dramas and later married him, had a cool and reserved style of beauty that contrasted well with the passionate Latin Lovers who were her leading men. They in-

cluded Ramon Novarro in *The Arab* (1924), Antonio Moreno in *Mare Nostrum* (1926) and Ivan Petrovich in *The Garden of Allah* (1927) and *The Three Passions* (1929).

Director King Vidor's wife Florence Vidor was ably directed by Lubitsch and Mal St Clair in many of the era's sophisticated comedies, and revealed real dramatic ability in *Alice Adams* (1923) and *Main Street* (1923), based on the novel in which Sinclair Lewis held up a mirror to prevailing middle-class values.

Joseph Schenck managed all three of the Talmadge sisters, who combined in one family three of the most popular heroine types of the day. Norma was the quintessential woman of the world, Constance was America's ideal of the giddy Flapper, and Natalie – who acted infrequently – was the conventional romantic heroine of the old school in films like *Our Hospitality* (1924).

The flapper-style heroines were perhaps the decade's most engaging stars, as personified by the young Joan Crawford, Gloria Swanson, Colleen Moore, Clara Bow, Louise Brooks, Sally O'Neil and Marion Davies. They clowned, danced, partied and pursued the good-looking men they admired in uninhibited style through any number of light-hearted vehicles like *Our Dancing Daughters* (1928), in which Crawford summed up the spirit of the Jazz Age in the line 'It feels so good – just to be alive!'

Gloria Swanson was the best known of this group, and one of the first to 'live like a star' in Hollywood. She became a Sennett Bathing Beauty by way of the Fox Sunshine Comedies and a series of dramas made for Triangle. Then De Mille enthroned her as the symbol of Jazz-Age verve and vitality in six comedies that made the most of her native wit and off-beat, exotic good looks. When her contract with Famous-Players Lasky came up for renewal, according to Jesse Lasky Jr, 'She was offered one million dollars a year, plus half the profits of any film she appeared in. It was the fattest offer ever made to any screen star – but it was not enough.' Swanson formed her own company, with financial backing from Boston business tycoon Joseph P Kennedy, and proceeded to produce her own pictures, playing not only flappers, but serious dramatic roles like *Sadie Thompson* (1928).

Child actress Clara Bow became an adult star when author Elinor Glyn – another outspoken redhead – picked her to star in *It* (1927), a contractual privilege rarely extended to writers. Glyn had been imported from England in 1921 by Jesse L Lasky Sr to write a torrid screenplay for the Gloria Swanson vehicle *The Great Moment* (1921), following upon the success of her risqué novel *Three Weeks* and others like it. According to Jesse L

Below: From left, Natalie, Constance and Norma Talmadge at one of Marion Davies' famous costume parties, this one with a kiddie theme.

Left: One-time cowboy Gary Cooper and friends on the set of *Morocco* (1930), directed by Josef von Sternberg.

Below: Child actress Clara Bow grew up to become the 'It' Girl in 1927, when Elinor Glyn cast her in the sex epic of the decade.

Lasky Jr, Glyn disembarked from the *Mauretania* in New York and almost stopped traffic with her exotic appearance: 'flaming red hair, green eyes, powder-white face, dripping with leopard skins, she looked more like one of her own heroines than an authoress.' Madame Glyn had very decided ideas about what constituted sex appeal, and Clara Bow, then a minor but talented actress playing waitresses, salesgirls and manicurists, met her standards and was lifted from obscurity into international fame as 'the It girl' in 1927.

It also featured a Montana-bred actor and former cowboy named Gary Cooper, who had been in Hollywood for several years without attracting undue notice. He had worked in two-reelers after a brief stint as a cartoonist. Then roles in *The Winning of Barbara Worth* (1926), *Children of Divorce* (1927) and *Arizona Bound* (1927) seemed to promise better things, but failed to bring stardom. Lasky reports that 'In those films, Gary Cooper had developed a direct, unactorish style that communicated a basic honesty. The strong, silent type. Few words – and important reaction close-ups.' Finally, Cooper's small part in *Wings* (1927) one of the first movies about aerial warfare in World War I, made an impact that led to a five-year contract with Famous Players Lasky. In *Whatever Happened to Hollywood*, Jesse L Lasky Jr recalls that '*Wings* was the last of the silent spectaculars and the first movie to win an Academy Award.' Richard Arlen, who began his acting career in *Wings*, said that 'We

spent six and a half months shooting it in San Antonio, Texas, using the entire United States Air Corps, which consisted of four pursuit planes. There was no trick photography. Buddy [Rogers] and I, who played young lieutenants, did our own flying.'

The popularity of Valentino gave rise to a series of Latin Lovers, including, briefly, Albert Valentino, who tried unsuccessfully to capitalize on his brother's success with several films made for FBC Productions in the late 1920s. Ramon Novarro did much better. He had already moved up from small roles into stardom in the *Prisoner of Zenda* (1922) before Metro signed him up for his dark good looks. His major films for that studio were *Scaramouche* (1923), *Ben Hur* (1926) and Lubitsch's *The Student Prince* (1928). Antonio Moreno brought an effective Latin touch to his roles opposite Clara Bow in *It* (1927), but he was no newcomer to Hollywood. He had been working in films since 1912, first as a popular serial star, then as a romantic leading man opposite Pola Negri in *The Spanish Dancer* (1923), Alice Terry in *Mare Nostrum* (1926) and Greta Garbo in *The Temptress* (1926). Another candidate in the Hollywood search for a new Valentino after the star's death was an amateur tango dancer whom Jesse L Lasky Sr discovered at the Cocoanut Grove. Upon learning that he bore the unsuitable name of Jack Krantz, Lasky rechristened him Ricardo Cortez and entered him in the Latin Lover sweepstakes, where he enjoyed success both as an actor and later as a director.

John Gilbert's appeal was also based partly on his dark good looks, although his origins were purely American. He was born John Pringle, in Logan, Utah, to a show-business family. His father was the owner and chief comic of the Pringle Stock Company. Gilbert gravitated naturally to Hollywood, where he worked for several years with Ince, both writing and acting, before he attracted major attention in *Monte Cristo* (1922). His very real talent resisted typecasting, and he distinguished himself in such disparate roles as the American boy in *The Big Parade* (1925), Rodolpho, opposite Lillian Gish, in *La Bohème* (1926) and the villainous Danilo in Stroheim's *The Merry Widow* (1925). Gilbert's name was linked romantically with that of Greta Garbo both on and off-screen. The love stories they made together, beginning with *Flesh and the Devil* (1927), helped reshape the image of the desirable male away from the Valentino model toward the all-American hero represented in the 1930s by Clark Gable and Gary Cooper.

In 1928 Gilbert was earning $10,000 a week at MGM. Then his career foundered in the film-industry revolution brought on by sound, and he struggled to get into directing, handicapped by debt, multiple marriages and a drinking problem that grew increasingly worse. Laurence Olivier described his third marriage, to Ina Claire, as 'an unkind, empty gesture on his part, taking advantage of a young female's flattered fascination simply in order to snap his fingers at her as he paraded her in front of Garbo.' Whether or not this is a fair assessment, there is no doubt that Gilbert never recovered emotionally from the collapse of his career. Charles Lockwood reports that 'Before Gilbert died of a heart attack at his Tower Grove Road home in 1936 at the age of forty-one, his alcoholic-induced delusions grew worse, and he started to believe that people were plotting against him.' David Niven corroborates the story that Gilbert's beautiful Beverly Hills home had become a 'somber place' before the actor's premature death: 'The decor was heavy, and the gloom of the place was intensified by curtains permanently drawn against the light.'

Of all the Latin-style lovers, Mexican-born Gilbert Roland seemed perhaps the most logical successor to the mantle of Valentino. But whether because he arrived on the scene after the Valentino craze had peaked, or because his roles were not suited to his talents, he did not achieve more than limited success during the silent period. Jesse L Lasky Jr reports that his screen name was formed by combining the names of the popular John Gilbert and Ruth Roland – and that 'His studio threatened to take back its name and send him back to being Luis Alonso when Gilbert Roland asked for a raise.'

Left: Clarence Brown directs John Gilbert and Greta Garbo in a love scene for *A Woman of Affairs* (1928). The real-life romance between two of Hollywood's most beautiful people was a factor in Garbo's aloofness from society.

Below: Pola Negri was imported by Paramount because of her success in German films and soon challenged Gloria Swanson's supremacy at the studio. Her well-publicized affair with Rudolph Valentino, however, alienated many of her fans.

The 1920s abounded in exotic leading ladies, many of them foreign-born, who complemented the exotic Valentino persona. The original vamp, of course, was Theda Bara, who was the product of Hollywood's first all-out public-relations campaign. Fox Studio reported to the press that Theda was the illegitimate daughter of a French artist and an Arabian princess, born in the shadow of an Egyptian pyramid, and that her name was an anagram for 'Arab Death.' Actually, she was born Theodosia Goodman, the daughter of a Cincinnati tailor; she migrated to Hollywood and worked as an extra until she was discovered in 1914. The following year, she became a star in the six-reel film *A Fool There Was*, based on the Rudyard Kipling poem about the deluded middle-aged civil servant and family man who is destroyed by a seductress – the vampire. In the final scene, Theda Bara, wearing a black velvet gown and pearls, idly tosses rose petals onto the body of her victim, who has fallen to his death through a stair railing after sacrificing career, family and self-respect to a few weeks on the Riviera with the temptress. This was heady stuff for the 1910s, and it created a box-office demand for vamp-style heroines that continued even after Bara's star set late in the decade.

The Polish actress Pola Negri was a logical successor to Theda Bara in both public and private life. She had been a theater actress of renown in both Warsaw and Germany, and her importation to America in 1922 was done with appropriate studio fanfare. Jesse L Lasky Jr reported that 'Pola Negri's' arrival could hardly have been topped by the Second Coming. Having been mobbed, by careful

prearrangement, at the dock, she was driven down Fifth Avenue to the old St Regis Hotel behind a police escort of screaming sirens, totally paralyzing the traffic. ... Having acquired honorary membership in several Indian tribes en route to Hollywood, she was somewhat disappointed with the film capital itself. Despite having received the by now traditional red-carpet reception at Pasadena, she described it as a "sleepy small town of squat, undistinguished buildings.'" Negri's reputation grew with her mid-1920s films, especially Mauritz Stiller's *Hotel Imperial* (1927), and her personal life was flamboyant enought to satisfy her fans. She married successively a Baron, a Count and a

Prince, and was linked romantically with both Charlie Chaplin and Valentino (at whose funeral she appeared in widow's weeds). She had a Roman pool installed in her Beverly Hills mansion and lived the star image to the hilt until the vamp character played itself out in the late 1920s, by which time, Lasky recalls 'Pola Negri . . . was giving stereotype performances in films that looked as though they were turned out by stamping machines. Perhaps it was the fault of bad scripts or misguided publicity – in any case, exhibitors were demanding that Negri's name be removed from the advertisements of her pictures! An investment in talent wasted, the movie queen returned to Europe to recapture her artistic integrity.'

Vilma Banky was another popular star in the vamp mode after her arrival from Hungary by way of the Austrian cinema to make two films with Valentino: *The Eagle* (1925) and *Son of the Sheik* (1926), the Italian idol's last picture. After his death, she played opposite the rising British actor Ronald Colman in several other films before her thick Hungarian accent ended her career early in the sound era, when studios became morbidly accent-conscious. (When Maurice Chevalier was hired in Paris by Famous Players-Lasky, the New York office wired frantically: URGE CANCEL CHEVALIER DEAL STOP PUBLIC WILL NOT REPEAT WILL NOT ACCEPT ACCENTS STOP EVEN RUTH CHATTERTON TOO ENGLISH FOR AMERICA STOP FRENCH ACCENT TEN TIMES WORSE STOP. Fortunately, this directive was ignored, and the business minds of the studio were glad to find themselves proved wrong.)

Another European import, Nita Naldi, enjoyed a brief reign as 'Queen of the Vampires' during her appearances opposite Valentino in *Blood and Sand* (1922), *A Sainted Devil* (1924) and *Cobra* (1925). Other vamps of the day were home-grown, including Barbara La Marr, who started life in Richmond, Virginia, as Rheatha Watson. During her brief heyday in the mid-1920s, when she starred in such costume epics as *The Three Musketeers* (1921) and *The Prisoner of Zenda* (1922), the exotic-looking young star had a sunken onyx bathtub with gold fixtures installed in her mansion and got married four times. (She had been married twice before coming to Hollywood.) But 'the Girl Who Was Too Beautiful,' as the newspapers described her, died in 1926 at the age of 29 from a drug overdose that the press reported as 'overdieting.' Two Mexican actresses appeared on the scene in the late 1920s and lasted well into the following decade. Lupe Velez brought a vital, tempestuous quality to her screen roles that carried over into her

Above: Buster Keaton's expressive face and vaudeville-trained skills made him one of the silent screen's best-loved comedians. His directorial abilities were equally impressive.

personal life. The beautiful Dolores Del Rio was brought to Hollywood by First National and enjoyed immediate popularity in such films as *What Price Glory* (1926) and *The Loves of Carmen* (1927).

Marie Dressler's career spanned three decades of film history, beginning during World War I, when she made several comedies based on her theatrical success in *Tillie's Nightmare*. Dressler returned to Hollywood in 1927 and took up a career as a character actress, which lasted well into the 1930s. She appeared frequently with Polly Moran, with whom she first played in *The Callaghans and the Murphys* (1927). Another transplanted stage performer was Louise Dresser, who began to work in films at the age of 40 and gave memorable performances in the silents *The Goose Woman* (1925) and *The Eagle* (1925), in which she played Catherine the Great. Later, she assumed the role of the Tsarina Elisabeth in Josef von Sternberg's *The Scarlet Empress*.

Of the great silent comedians, three of the greatest were also directors, two of them – Chaplin and Keaton – among the masters. As David Robinson has pointed out: 'Chaplin's unique spell upon the audiences of the whole world guaranteed him the possibility of complete independence, which he seized and

maintained. Keaton, until he was crushed in the rapidly growing organisational machinery of the late silent period, was profitable enough to be supported in comparative independence by the industry.' Both began their careers on the stage, Chaplin in the music halls of London and Keaton in his family's vaudeville act, in which he appeared from the age of three. Chaplin's deprived childhood and youth gave him unusual insight into the situation of the underprivileged, which emerged in his beloved tramp-clown character, called by Robinson 'the one universal symbol created by the cinema in its first half-century . . . With one notable exception, Chaplin's films of the postwar decade are variations on the theme of the tramp clown – the Universal Everyman – cast into different, recognisable human situations.' *Shoulder Arms* (1918), released three weeks before the Armistice that ended World War I, remains 'the most durable of all the many films made about that war.' *The Kid* (1921), with Jackie Coogan, grossed over two and a half million dollars for First National, which released it. Of the Chaplin comedies released through United Artists, *The Gold Rush* (1925), *The Circus* (1928) and *City Lights* (1931) were among the most memorable.

Chaplin's turbulent and highly publicized private life provided endless copy for the Hollywood press, beginning with his forced marriage to 16-year-old Lita Grey, who became pregnant during her role in *The Gold Rush*. Two years later, Grey's 52-page Bill of Divorcement was made public by the Los Angeles papers under the title *Complaint by Lita Grey*: the mildest accusations lodged against the prominent actor and director were 'cheapness, spying on her, asking her to have an abortion, changing all the house locks, extreme cruelty, and carrying on an affair with "a certain prominent moving picture actress."' Later, Grey's uncle threatened to reveal the names of not one but five actresses with whom Chaplin had allegedly been involved during his marriage. To avoid the implication of these other five women in the case, Chaplin settled for a payment of $625,000 to his former wife and agreed to her custody of their two sons, Charles Jr and Sydney Earle Chaplin. Each child received a $100,000 trust fund, and with attorneys' fees, the divorce cost Chaplin over a million dollars and damaged his reputation with his public for years thereafter.

Keaton's skills for improvising and developing comic business were honed in the demanding school of vaudeville, long before his friend Roscoe Arbuckle invited him to 'come on down to the studio Monday and do a scene with me or two and see how you like it.' The result was *The Butcher Boy* (1917) –

Far left and left: The passionate artistry of London-born Charlie Chaplin made him a towering figure in the industry, both as director and actor. Film historian David Robinson has called Chaplin's immortal tramp-clown character 'the one universal symbol created by the cinema in its first half-century.'

an immediate hit with audiences. Although he was nicknamed 'the Great Stone Face,' Keaton had, in fact, one of the most expressive faces in films. And he was as athletic and agile as Douglas Fairbanks – able to leap, somersault and fall off a cliff with equal ease. Unlike Chaplin, Keaton played a different character in every film, including his great *The Three Ages* (1923) and *The Cameraman* (1928). As Robinson observes, 'The characteristic Keaton plot situation confronts the unaided and strictly human hero with some vast problem and then sets him to discover the solution.' And so he did, both in art and in life, throughout over a decade of film-making.

After Keaton left Arbuckle to form his own production company in 1920, he developed his own taut style and typical gags like the comedian's encounter with intransigent objects and forces of nature – do-it-yourself house construction kits, home-made boats that pulled down the foundations of the house when launched from their cellar construction site; rivers, and trains. *The Navigator* (1924) set a young millionaire couple adrift on an otherwise-deserted ocean liner, and *Seven Chances* (1925) gave its hero 24 hours to find a bride so that he could inherit a fortune. Keaton's *The General* (1926), based on a real episode of the American Civil War, remains the masterpiece of silent-film comedy.

Keaton's success led to a $300,000 house in Beverly Hills, built at the urging of his wife Natalie Talmadge, who wanted to live on a scale appropriate to his early-1920s income of several thousand dollars a week. (It was reported that when he showed guests around the new Italian-style villa, he sometimes remarked: 'It took a lot of pratfalls, my friends, to build this dump.') As actress Louise Brooks observed later, 'Buster's whole life then was a movie. His house was a set, the swimming pool was a set, the barbecue pit was a set.' Sadly, the expensive estate behind the Beverly Hills Hotel went on the market after Keaton's career succumbed to his company's absorption by MGM and his marriage ended in estrangement.

Keaton's mentor in the film business was slapstick comedian Roscoe Arbuckle, a product of Keystone Studios, where his wife, Minta Durfee, also became an actress. As she recalled years later for Walter Wagner, 'Mr Sennett had teamed Roscoe with Mabel Normand, and they were the most perfect combination the world ever knew. They were terrific working together as a comedy team, and the audiences loved them.' After four years with Sennett, Arbuckle went to Paramount with an unprecedented contract for $3,000,000 a year.

Like Chaplin, Arbuckle had grown up in

Below: The silent-comedy team of Fatty Arbuckle and Mabel Normand in Mack Sennett's *He Did and He Didn't* (1916).

poverty, and during his early years in Hollywood, his wife recalled, 'He spent money wildly. He was the first star to have the entourage. Roscoe bought me a Rolls-Royce, the first one in Hollywood, with a genuine silver radiator. And jewels, my darling, like you've never seen. He was the most generous man on earth … We toured the world, went to China and Europe, and for a cross-country trip to promote one of Roscoe's new pictures. Evalyn Walsh McLean, the woman who owned the Hope diamond, lent us her private train. We stopped in twenty-three cities, and every place we went the crowds came out to cheer and greet us.'

Minta Durfee Arbuckle blamed the Hearst press for the scandal-mongering publicity that wrecked her husband's career after the celebrated accusation of manslaughter in the death of Virginia Rappe. Although he was found not guilty in three separate trials, 'Hollywood was closed to him because the women's clubs and the Legion of Decency were still out for Roscoe's scalp … About all that happened was that Jack Warner let him direct three shorts, and Roscoe couldn't even use his own name. The name he did use was sad and heartbreaking: Will B. Good.'

Wallace Beery made a transition from roles as the heavy in his early career to the 'lovable rogue' type that he played in *The Pony Express* (1925) and his later sound films. And the 'Our Gang' comedies produced by Hal Roach Sr were a training ground for numerous comedians, including Jackie Coogan and later, in the 1930s, Carl Switzer, Billy Thomas and Darla Hood. After Roach sold 'the Gang' to MGM, Hood and other members of the young troupe moved to the Metro lot, which she remembers as 'a wonderland. When we weren't working, we were allowed to go round to all the sets. They were making Tarzan out there at the time, and we got to play on that set. And there was the Andy Hardy house and the train station where Mickey Rooney always said good-bye to his folks or to his girl friend Polly Benedict when he was going on a trip. And I remember watching them shoot *The Wizard of Oz*.'

Greta Garbo made 10 silent films in Hollywood and moved effortlessly into the sound medium for additional triumphs, beginning with *Anna Christie* (1930), when advertisements trumpeted 'Garbo Speaks!' Louis B Mayer had brought her to Hollywood along with Mauritz Stiller, whose directorial skills transformed the shy and awkward Swedish girl into the world's greatest actress. As Jack Lodge observes, 'Through all of her American career she made no film away from MGM, and the reward of that loyalty was that she had the best the studio could offer – the best in sets and costumes, a variety of serviceable stories, the camerawork of William Daniels, the direction of Clarence Brown, who made five of her thirties films, and of such fine stylists as Edmund Goulding, George Fitzmaurice, and Rouben Mamoulian. Garbo was always herself, serene, secret, lit from within.' With *Anna Karenina* (1935), *Camille* (1936), and *Conquest* (1937) her position as the world's reigning film actress was unchallenged.

Garbo's desire for privacy was legendary, and corroborated by all those who did get to know the reclusive Swedish star during her years in Hollywood. She insisted that Bill Daniels photograph all her pictures at MGM, and he recalled that 'She could sniff an outsider a mile away, and if anyone, no matter whom, came on the set to get a peek at her, she'd sense it even with a couple hundred extras around and she'd just go and sit in her dressing room till they'd been put out.' David Niven tells the story of how Groucho Marx learned not to intrude upon the reserved Garbo one day when the extroverted comedian 'saw a well-known figure approaching in slacks and floppy hat. He waylaid her, bent down in his famous crouch, and peeked up under the brim. Two prisms of pure Baltic blue stared down at him, and he backed away, muttering, "Pardon me, ma'am. I thought you were a guy I knew in Pittsburgh."'

Of the much-publicized Garbo/Gilbert love affair, Niven reflects that it was 'too highly publicized perhaps for Garbo's taste, because at the very moment when Gilbert thought that all was set for a wedding and a honeymoon in the South Pacific aboard a yacht specially and romantically outfitted for the occasion, Garbo had taken to her heels.

Gilbert, thereafter, married twice elsewhere, but both marriages fell apart.' The two remained close to the end of Gilbert's life, but friends on Summit Drive, including Ronald Colman and David O Selznick, rarely caught a glimpse of Garbo except on her solitary walks in the nearby hills, 'when Jack was drinking.'

Above: The serene and flawless beauty of Greta Garbo made the great Swedish actress a legend in her own time.

Left: The Jackie Coogan home in Los Angeles, purchased with the earnings of the popular child star (standing on running board) whose first major film was *The Kid* with Charlie Chaplin (1920). His parents' appropriation of his $4 million-dollar income as a child star led to extensive lawsuits and ultimately resulted in the Coogan Act, which was designed to protect the interests of other child wage-earners.

Above: German-born Marlene Dietrich, the protegée of director Josef von Sternberg, came to Hollywood at the behest of Paramount Pictures and enjoyed enormous success during the 1930s.

Garbo's career continued into the war years, when she chose abruptly to retire after the failure of the farcical *Two-Faced Woman* (1941), which Niven described as 'a four-star, fur-lined, oceangoing disaster. Nothing in show business is more horrendous than a farce when it is not funny. It also contained a surprising quota of "dirty" dialogue, was banned by the Legion of Decency, and roasted by the press, with one eminent reviewer referring to Garbo's appearance as "embarrassing – like seeing Sarah Bernhardt swatted with a bladder."' Undoubtedly, Garbo could have recovered easily from this setback, but she simply stopped making films and retired to New York, returning occasionally to 'haunt Hollywood like a lovely ghost,' as Niven described it.

Another megastar of the 1930s was the glamourous Marlene Dietrich, whose first big film was *The Blue Angel* (1930), made in her native Germany with director Josef von Sternberg, who also directed six of her first seven American pictures after Paramount imported the new international star to Hollywood. As Jack Lodge has written, 'Seldom have the careers of a star and a director been so closely interwoven. Sternberg's genius was for the pictorial; a master of lighting, as well as of design, he filled his movies with one harmonious, richly decorated composition after another, with the focal point always his star. A lesser actress might have become part of Sternberg's set, as lovely

and as lavishly adorned as the rest ... But with Dietrich it was not so.'

American audiences were enthralled by the beautiful German star in movies like *Shanghai Express* (1932) and *The Scarlet Empress* (1934). In *Whatever Happened to Hollywood*, Jesse L Lasky describes the party given by his father to welcome Dietrich to the United States after she signed with Paramount. 'Earthy, lusty, yet mysteriously sophisticated, the lady swaggered into the crowded room ... bringing a breath of continental bistros, exotic places. She had a certain sloe-eyed magnetism that years and time would never dim. From head to toe she was a star, loaded with that particular magic that stars exude.'

According to Lasky, 'She arrived complete with, so rumor had it, lover and husband,' and speculation was rife as to which was which. 'The golden-blond, blue-eyed young Teutonic athlete who might have stepped out of a Wagnerian opera, brimming with virility and bronzed from some Alpine ski slope, was her husband, Rudolph Sieber. The caved-in, disheveled, unkempt, gnomelike von Sternberg was her admirer and discoverer. A Hollywood cliche was shattered.'

Katharine Hepburn, who would not reach the height of her popularity until the 1940s, when she left RKO for MGM and her partnership with Spencer Tracy, attracted an early following with such films as *Morning Glory* (1933). Hepburn was not cast in the typical film-star mold. Although strikingly beautiful, she came across to some as too highbrow, with her high-pitched, cultured voice and unmistakable intelligence. Jack Lodge notes that 'At another studio she might have been groomed into a semblance of convention. At RKO, the studio's weakness for the wayward, and even bizarre, was the very thing needed to engage her formidable talent.'

Hepburn's 1930s successes included *Alice Adams* (1935), based on the Booth Tarkington novel about a small-town girl with intellectual and social pretensions, *Sylvia Scarlett* (1934), *Stage Door* (1937), *Bringing Up Baby* (1938), the delightful comedy with Cary Grant, and *Mary of Scotland* (1936). On loan to Columbia, she appeared again with Grant to play the eccentric daughter of a stuffy family in *Holiday* (1938), well supported by Jean Dixon and Edward Everett Horton. Two years later, she entered the new decade with one of her best films, the engaging *The Philadelphia Story* (1940).

Beautiful Kay Francis was enormously popular in the early 1930s in such films as *Ladies' Man* (1931), *Cynara* (1932) and *Trouble in Paradise* (1932). After Marlene Dietrich's arrival at Paramount, Francis moved to Warners, where she made her finest

Above: The unconventional style of Katharine Hepburn, seen with Cary Grant, combined brains and beauty and engendered a successful career that began in the early 1930s and has continued to the present day. Her relaxed manner also foreshadowed a change in behavior that is still evident.

film, *One Way Passage* with William Powell, in 1932. Norma Shearer was another leading lady whose lack of striking beauty was offset by strong acting skills and good casting and direction under the aegis of her husband, MGM's brilliant head of production, Irving Thalberg. Their marriage was one of Hollywood's few romantic success stories, and lasted from 1927 until Thalberg's death of pneumonia in 1936.

Joan Crawford's popularity began in the

silent era and continued through the 1930s and into the war years. She was often typecast as the ambitious working girl – a more mature version of her urgent portrayals of the Jazz Age flapper – and her best 1930s films were *Grand Hotel* (1932) and *The Women* (1939), which gave greater scope to her real ability. Her personal life was stormy and well publicized, including four marriages, numerous love affairs, and disputes with fellow workers and studio heads.

Charles Lockwood reports in *Dream Palaces* that during the early 1930s, Crawford retained Hollywood decorator and former film star William Haines to redecorate her Brentwood home, shortly before her divorce from Douglas Fairbanks Jr. 'Haines promptly got rid of the kitschy 1920s furniture that she had bought in the first flush of her stardom several years earlier. Afterward,

Left: The perennial Joan Crawford strikes a narcissistic pose beside the swimming pool at her Brentwood Heights house in 1940.

the drawing room – that's what Joan insisted on calling the living room – was painted white with Wedgwood-blue trim … The former dining room became the music room, where Joan occasionally played records of her singing opera to tensely smiling guests … Several years later, she adopted Christina, the first of the four children she raised behind the masonry wall encircling her home at 426 North Bristol Circle. Today her former Brentwood mansion is known as the "Mommie Dearest House."'

Jean Harlow, another graduate of the Sennett comedy school, was making several hundred dollars a week as a starlet when she attracted major attention in *Hell's Angels* (1930). The following year, *Platinum Blonde* (1931), directed by Frank Capra, confirmed her new status. Jesse L Lasky Jr recorded that 'She filled the eye and imagination with the impact of her looks and personality. I never saw a star with more personal magnetism. Many had it on screen, brought to life by the camera, like fireflies ignited to view by darkness. They needed the attentions of makeup people, wardrobe, and finally a director to supply the spark that came through the camera's eye. Not so Jean Harlow.'

Below: The vibrant Jean Harlow at the height of her career in the early 1930s. Her star-crossed personal life never affected the quality of her performances or the personal magnetism that made her one of Hollywood's best-liked celebrities.

Near the peak of her career, Harlow faced the shock of her second husband, Paul Bern's, suicide and the attendant scandal. Lasky says that 'No one who knew her really doubted her innocence,' but the Los Angeles police were dissatisfied with Bern's ambiguous suicide note to his wife and 'Only the desperate efforts of L B Mayer and his great publicity chief prevented her being indicted on a murder charge.' Harlow was at this time only in her early twenties. Then *Red Dust* (1932), with Clark Gable, and *Bombshell* (1933) brought her to new heights of popularity. 'Ahead lay a third marriage to Harold Rossen, the great cameraman, which would end unsuccessfully, and the famous romance with Bill Powell,' recalls Lasky, who dated Harlow himself for a time. He was shocked by the news of her death at the age of 26, which he read in the newspapers on his way back from a trip to Europe. 'The generally accepted cause of Jean's death was a uremic infection brought on by the powerful hair bleach she used. Norman Zierold, Boswell of *The Hollywood Tycoons*, blamed her mother, who, a Christian Scientist, had failed to summon medical aid until too late.' An only-in-Hollywood footnote to the sad story is the real-estate ad that appeared shortly before the star's death, when she was plagued by money problems and had to sell her Beverly Glen estate: 'Glamour Star's New Ancestral Mansion for Sale.'

Janet Gaynor continued into the 1930s the successful career that had brought her the first-ever Best Actress award from the Academy of Motion Picture Arts and Sciences in 1928. Her delicate beauty and sensitive portrayals made her a favorite with audiences, especially in the romantic comedies that she did so well. Her last picture before her retirement was *The Young In Heart* (1938), in which she played one of a charming family of confidence men and women who come to see the error of their ways.

Jean Arthur was another ebullient comedy star who brought not only warmth and a sense of fun to her roles but a degree of shrewd realism as well. Her career had taken off in 1929, when the Western Association of Motion Picture Advertisers chose her as that year's 'Wampas Baby Star.' This coveted award of merit by a group of studio publicity men was a passport to success in the amount of newspaper and magazine space it generated. Others who profited from the accolade during the Glamour Years were Bessie Love, Laura La Plante, Clara Bow, Mary Astor, Dolores De Rio, Joan Crawford, Lupe Velez, Loretta Young and Joan Blondell.

The irresistible 1930s touch with sophisticated comedy also showcased the talents of Claudette Colbert, whose effervescence carried her through numerous popular films, including the wayward adventure story *It Happened One Night* (1934), with Clark Gable. The familiar reporter-meets-rich-girl theme was lifted from mediocrity by Gable's flawless performance as the cynical reporter, Colbert's unflagging vitality and charm, and delightful support from Roscoe Karns, Ward Bond and Walter Connolly. The film collected all four major Oscars: Best Film, Director, Actor and Actress – a feat unmatched until four decades later.

Once Paramount perceived Carole Lombard's gift for comedy, she too became a popular fixture as a fey, scatter-brained and off-beat heroine of popular romantic comedies like *No Man of Her Own* (1932) with Gable. Their off-screen romance flourished long before their marriage in 1939. The athletic Lombard matched the hard-playing Gable drink for drink, and the two regularly hunted, rode and camped together until Lombard's death in a plane crash three years after their marriage.

Among male stars of the 1930s, Gable was the undisputed king, and this was his nick-

Above: Charles Laughton, Carole Lombard and Gary Cooper relaxing while filming at Paramount in 1934.

Left: Frank Capra directing a scene for the blockbuster comedy *It Happened One Night*, with Claudette Colbert and Clark Gable.

Right: Clark Gable on the set of *San Francisco* (1936), directed by W S Van Dyke.

Below: Wallace Beery looks stumped during a card game with Jean Harlow, Clark Gable and Mary Carlyle, played between takes of the 1931 gangster film *The Secret Six.*

name, not only at MGM, but throughout the film community. His first big picture was *A Free Soul* (1931), in which he played a gangster and almost stole the film from Norma Shearer and Leslie Howard. That same year he played opposite Greta Garbo in *Susan Lenox: Her Fall and Rise.* Then came *Red Dust* (1932), the steamy jungle adventure with Jean Harlow that was later remade as *Mogambo* (1954). As his popularity in-

creased, MGM moved Gable out of the heavy role into more sympathetic parts, with varying success. In *Idiot's Delight* (1939), for example, he was badly miscast, and *Parnell* (1937) was not his best vehicle. But his box-office appeal was not damaged by these exceptions to his generally excellent portrayals, and in *Gone With The Wind* (1939) he scored his major film triumph.

Ann Rutherford recalled of their days at MGM together that 'Clark Gable was the warmest, best-liked person on the set. He was adored by everyone who came in contact with him.' Rutherford played Careen O'Hara in *Gone With The Wind,* and claimed that 'From the very first day of shooting there was an electricity that permeated the atmosphere on the set. We knew we were part of something very special ... When the picture opened in 1939, I went to all four premieres, Los Angeles, Chicago, New York and Atlanta. In Atlanta I rode with Mr Selznick to the airport to meet Clark and Carole. Mr Selznick wanted to hug himself with glee because he had pulled it off and he knew he had a winner.'

Gone With The Wind was, of course, made by independent producer David O Selznick after he left Paramount. Jesse L Lasky Jr recalls that 'Louis B Mayer had acquired a film giant for a son-in-law' in the person of Selznick, who married Irene Mayer, the boss's daughter. 'Later, when he set up to produce independently, Mayer made it a condition of loaning him Clark Gable for *Gone With The Wind* that the film would be released through MGM. So in 1939 MGM had got itself the biggest money-maker in

Left: Ronald Colman, right, and Donald Woods are the center of attention as Jack Conway directs the tavern scene adapted from Dickens' classic *A Tale of Two Cities* (1935), in which Colman played the noble Sydney Carton and Woods Charles Darnay.

Hollywood history without having had to invest a penny of its own money.'

The handsome British actor Ronald Colman retained the silent-screen popularity he enjoyed in films like *Stella Dallas* (1925) and *Beau Geste* (1926) into the new decade. Sound only enhanced his appeal, as he had a mellifluous stage-trained voice. Colman was a sophisticated romantic hero in such adventures as *The Prisoner of Zenda* (1937) with Madeleine Carroll – the remake of a silent film. Audiences wept over his noble Sydney Carton in *A Tale of Two Cities* (1935) and applauded his dashing François Villon in *If I Were King* (1938).

David Niven, a close friend of Colman's, recalled that, like Garbo, 'He had a mania for preserving his privacy – understandable really when one remembers that on any given day, hundreds of fans would be cruising, goggle-eyed, around Beverly Hills in limousines, jalopies or buses equipped with loudspeakers ... Important putts on the greens of the Bel Air Country Club were frequently muffed by prominent local citizens, thanks to a blaring voice from the nearby road describing their distant clubhouse as "the palatial home of the beautiful platinum bombshell – Jean Harlow ... where champagne flows and anything goes."'

Colman was particularly reticent after the collapse of his unhappy first marriage, but his romance with Benita Hume helped overcome his natural reserve and resulted in a happier second marriage. Niven was a frequent guest at Colman's Summit Drive home, where

'Christmas dinner was a permanent fixture. On went the dinner jackets, down went the turkey, plum pudding and champagne, and out poured the speeches.'

Another frequent guest was Douglas Fairbanks Jr, whose mother was the senior Fairbanks' first wife, Beth Sully. Douglas Fairbanks Sr objected strongly to his son's becoming an actor, but 'Eventually, when my luck changed and I was able to stand on my own feet and achieve a certain modest success, he was the first to tell everybody in the most generous terms that I had done it on my own, without any help from him.' Douglas

Below: C Henry Gordon, left, as Surat Khan, and Errol Flynn, playing Major Geoffrey Vickers, rehearse their lines for a scene in *The Charge of the Light Brigade* (1936), directed by Michael Curtiz, right. Dialogue director Irving Rapper holds the script.

Fairbanks Jr was both a stage and screen star. He made over 75 films, including those he remembered most fondly from the 1930s: *Dawn Patrol* (1930), *Catherine the Great* (1933), *Prisoner of Zenda* (1937) and *Gunga Din* (1939). 'Whatever I achieved,' he told Walter Wagner much later, 'was by sheer drive and necessity . . . I would rather have been something else than a film star.' But despite his reluctance, Fairbanks was one of the most attractive and popular stars of his day.

Errol Flynn made his mark in Hollywood shortly after his arrival as an unknown contract player for Warner Brothers, who advertised him as an Irish actor 'straight from a successful career with the Abbey Players.' Actually, he was Australian by birth, and had been brought up in Tasmania and New Guinea, as his friend David Niven recalled in *Bring on the Empty Horses*. The two were roommates for a while after Flynn's tempestuous relationship with Lili Damita broke up. Flynn's reputation as a roistering womanizer and hard-drinking bar fighter was not manufactured by the Hollywood press. As Niven put it, 'Humility was a word unknown to Errol. He became a big star overnight with his first Hollywood superproduction, *Captain Blood*, but it never crossed his mind that others . . . might have had a hand in

his success. It all went straight to his head.'

Flynn's second hit movie was *The Charge of the Light Brigade* (1936), in which Niven also appeared, and the two nearly ended their new-found careers in a bizarre near-accident during the filming. As Niven described it, 'Toward the end of the picture Errol and I were placed in a large basket atop an elephant; for some obscure reason Warner Brothers had decided to twist history and to let the Light Brigade charge across the North-West Frontier of India instead of the Russian Crimea. The scriptwriters had been ordered to insert a tiger hunt into the proceedings to warm things up, and we were shooting this sequence at the studio instead of in open country. This proved just as well because the elephant, driven mad by the arc lights and the megaphone, went berserk and dashed madly all over the back lot trying to scrape off the basket with us inside it against trees, archways, and the side of the fire station. Studio workers scattered like chaff as we trampled and trumpeted our way toward the main entrance, and only the astute closing of the gates by the studio police stopped us from careering out into the traffic of Pico Boulevard and heading for the Punjab.' Flynn's whole career was characterized by color and flamboyance, and his legendary exploits with women gave rise to the popular expression 'in like Flynn.'

Another Warner Brothers actor of the early 1930s was the young Spencer Tracy, who played mainly rough and rugged roles until he moved to MGM in 1935. Then his image underwent the change that marked his subsequent career as the reliable, steadfast and paternal hero of such films as *San Francisco* (1936) and *Boys' Town* (1938). *San Francisco*, in which he appeared with Clark Gable, was one of the biggest hits of 1936, with its stunning climax of the great earthquake and fire of 1906 (the special effects were by Arnold Gillespie).

Jeanette MacDonald was another star of *San Francisco* – and of the decade. She had been discovered in a Shubert musical in the late 1920s and appeared in several of the first film musicals when sound came in, notably opposite Maurice Chevalier in *The Love Parade* (1929). Her 1930s career at MGM brought the popular operettas that she made with Nelson Eddy, including *Naughty Marietta* (1935).

Most male heroes of the 1930s were known for their smoothness and charm – qualities that became increasingly important as the decade wore on. Even Jimmy Cagney moved away from his original tough-guy image and became more of a man about town. The trend was personified in such attractive and capable actors as William Powell, Robert Montgo-

Below: Australian-born Errol Flynn was an avid sailor and fisherman in his leisure hours.

mery, Franchot Tone, Robert Taylor, Robert Young and Melvyn Douglas. Cary Grant took the quality a step further.

Grant's career began at Paramount, where he was overshadowed by the sultry glamour of Marlene Dietrich in *Blonde Venus* (1932) and by the whirlwind style of Mae West in 1933's *She Done Him Wrong* and *I'm No Angel*. But these pictures garnered attention for the quiet, good-looking young actor, and he moved to RKO and Columbia, specializing first in the screwball comedies of the day. His talent made itself increasingly felt in such vehicles as *The Awful Truth* (1937), with Irene Dunne and Ralph Bellamy, and in *Bringing Up Baby* with Katharine Hepburn

in 1938. *Only Angels Have Wings* (1939) marked his full emergence into the ambivalent, sensitive hero that he would play in the Hitchcock films of the 1940s. Popular Grant films of the early 1940s included *His Girl Friday*, *The Philadelphia Story* and *Woman of the Year*.

After an unimpressive start in films, Humphrey Bogart had returned to the stage, where he starred in Robert E Sherwood's *The Petrified Forest* in 1934. Warner Brothers brought him back to Hollywood to play Duke Mantee, the killer on the run, in their film version of the play, which was highly praised; Leslie Howard and Bette Davis were featured with him. The following year, 1937,

Below left: Spencer Tracy (right) and Robert Young at lunch on location in Payette Lake, Idaho, for the 1939 film *Northwest Passage.*

Below: Cary Grant relaxes at his piano during his early years with Paramount.

Above: Fred and Phyllis Astaire with their son and daughter at the family vacation home, Chatsworth Ranch.

Right: Bette Davis, gowned for her role in *Kid Galahad* (1937), takes advantage of a break in filming with her knitting.

Below: Humphrey Bogart and his third wife, Mayo Methot, get ready to embark on their yacht, *Sluggy*, with their scotty, also called Sluggy, in tow.

Bogart appeared in *Black Legion*, one of Hollywood's rare political movies of the time, in which he gave a moving performance as a working man passed over for promotion who resorts to joining a right-wing 'America first' organization modeled on the Klu Klux Klan. That year brought six other popular Bogart films, including *Dead End* and *Marked Woman*, again with Bette Davis. The following year, *Angels with Dirty Faces* (1939), costarring James Cagney, merged social conscience with the electric vitality of the gangster genre at its best.

It was in 1938 that Bogart married the hard-drinking Mayo Methot, to form the couple that would become known to all Hollywood as 'the Battling Bogarts.' David Niven recalls the night on the town that 'I was sitting in a corner with the "Oomph Girl," Ann Sheridan, Bogie with Mayo a few tables away ... Suddenly all hell broke loose.' A drunken patron had poked Bogart in the chest and his wife hit the aggressor on his head with her shoe. 'I caught a momentary glimpse of flinty-eyed characters rising purposefully from the table whence the large man had come, and of a solid phalanx of waiters converging on the battle area. Cries of rage and alarm rose on all sides, and the air became thick with flying bottles, plates, glasses, left hooks and food. "Quick," screamed the Oomph Girl. "Under the table." We had not been installed there for more than a few seconds before Bogie came padding in on all fours; he was laughing like hell.'

Eventually, the battling Bogarts parted, and Bogart met Lauren (Betty) Bacall when she was 19 years old and he 44; the unknown model had been chosen to star opposite him in *To Have and Have Not* (1944). Their subsequent marriage ended only with his death 11 years later – long after he had broken out of the gangster mold foisted upon him in the late 1930s to star in such film classics as *The Maltese Falcon* (1941) and *Casablanca* (1942).

Bette Davis was a determined Broadway actress who crashed Hollywood in the early years of talking pictures and made up for her lack of striking physical beauty by sheer skill and drive. Despite the fact that Universal's Carl Laemmle Jr described her as having 'as much sex appeal as Slim Summerville,' audiences responded to her magnetic and thoroughly professional acting. In 1935 she won her first Academy Award as Best Actress for *Dangerous*. Three years later, she captured the prize again for her performance as a headstrong Southern beauty in *Jezebel*, opposite Henry Fonda. Ultimately, her Hollywood career would include over 80 pictures, including the great *Dark Victory* in 1939.

Fred Astaire had also been a Broadway star (since 1917), but during the early 1930s he made only one film, *Dancing Lady* (1933). Ginger Rogers had a longer career in films: her role in *42nd Street* (1933) was the culmination of four years in which she played leads in small pictures and supporting roles in larger ones. When the two discovered each other, the musical took wings. Astaire and Rogers danced in 10 RKO musicals, beginning with their supporting roles in *Flying Down to Rio* (1933). The movie is remembered best for its concluding aerial ballet on the wings of planes in flight and for the 'Carioca' number in which Astaire and Rogers started writing a new chapter in film history.

Romantic elegance had full play in the

Astaire-Rogers vehicles, and the couple's delightful dancing was enhanced by the rare chemistry between them. Everything worked right in their pictures: music, direction, sets, casting. Unforgettable numbers include Cole Porter's 'Night and Day' from *The Gay Divorcee* (1934), Jerome Kern's 'Lovely to Look At' from *Roberta* (1935) and 'The Way You Look Tonight' in *Swing Time* (1936). Perhaps the best loved of all is Irving Berlin's 'Let's Face the Music and Dance' from *Follow the Fleet* (1936). Rogers' down-to-earth approach was the perfect anchor for Astaire's more wayward flights, and audiences kept coming back for more until the pair decided to end their professional partnership in the late 1930s. As their friend and colleague David Niven concluded, 'Fred went on from strength to strength with a series of different dancing partners and Ginger decided to return to straight acting,' her first appearance being in Garson Kanin's *Bachelor Mother* (1938), in which Niven costarred. Niven was also a neighbor of Fred Astaire and his wife Phyllis, who constituted one of Hollywood's happiest and most enduring couples.

Child stars came into their own in the 1930s, when Shirley Temple was voted 'the most popular player on the screen today' by *Silver Screen* readers of 1935. Temple was immensely popular with audiences for her unaffected appeal in such films as *Little Miss Marker* (1934), *Stand Up and Cheer* (1934),

Above: Ginger Rogers rehearsing for *Swingtime* (1936) with Hermes Pan, who helped choreograph many of the Astaire-Rogers musicals.

Right: Shirley Temple takes an order from Adolph Zukor at the Paramount Cafe, as Cecil B De Mille looks on – 1936.

Above: The star-studded MGM commissary during the 1930s.

The Littlest Rebel (1935) and many others. Elizabeth Taylor was an immediate success in *National Velvet* (1944), and Mickey Rooney's Andy Hardy series not only made a great deal of money for MGM but served as a showcase for new talent, including Esther Williams, Donna Reed, Lana Turner and Judy Garland. Ann Rutherford, who co-starred with Rooney in the Hardy series as his girl friend Polly Benedict, claimed that 'They were the largest grossers that MGM ever made.' After her success in the Hardy series and *The Wizard of Oz* (1939), Judy Garland had a 10-room house built for her mother in newly fashionable Bel Air. She was then 17 years old.

Jesse L Lasky Jr was a scriptwriter at MGM during the late Glamour Years, and he recalled the studio's crowded commissary during the 'vintage year' of 1941. 'You could have seen picking at their salads Jimmy Stewart, Hedy Lamarr (in a sarong for *White Cargo*), Greer Garson, Lionel Barrymore, Katharine Hepburn, Irene Dunne, Red Skelton, William Powell, Wallace Beery, Spencer Tracy, Walter Pidgeon, Robert Taylor, Lewis Stone, Gene Kelly, George Murphy, Van Johnson, Marsha Hunt, Robert Benchley, Dame May Whitty, Esther Williams – a terrycloth robe covering her sleek bathing suit; Mary Astor (whose name my father had invented); June Allyson, the eternal girl next door; Spring Byington, Gladys Cooper, Barry Nelson, Desi Arnaz, and so many others!' From his long perspective on film history, Lasky added that 'If I had to select Hollywood's greatest period I suppose that this would have been it. Every studio grinding out hits, like *Mrs. Miniver, Good-bye Mr Chips, A Woman's Face, Waterloo Bridge, Dr. Jekyll and Mr. Hyde, The Grapes of Wrath.* Stars were earning their top salaries, pampered, protected, and groomed by the executives, who regarded them as priceless commodities.' Hollywood had come a long way from the days when Mary Pickford was billed only as 'the Biograph girl,' and, as she recalled, 'The exhibitors didn't know my name, and of course, neither did the public.'

'EVERYBODY THAT'S ANYBODY...'

Long before the watershed year of 1940, the word 'Hollywood' no longer referred to a geographic entity, but to a gigantic industry that had an enormous impact on the manners and mores of the world. The handful of film pioneers who had made their way to the bucolic community outside Los Angeles had grown into a full-fledged subculture, with its own language, laws, economy, communications system and way of life. The luxurious homes of movie stars and tycoons dotted the San Fernando Valley, Bel Air and Brentwood. Studios had sprung up from Burbank to Culver City. Exotic hotels, country clubs and night spots vied for the patronage of the rich and famous, whose activities Middle America followed with breathless interest through the gossip columns and fan magazines. Few could have guessed in 1940 that the Glamour Years were almost over.

The premiere event of the New Year's social whirl was the opening of entrepreneur Billy Wilkerson's newest and most grandiose venture on the site of the old Club Seville. Wilkerson spared no expense on his new enterprise, and generated public excitement through his *Hollywood Reporter*. 'Everybody that's anybody will be at Ciro's' trumpeted the daily ads prior to the grand opening. When first-nighters flocked to the impressively modern building at 8433 Sunset, with its facade designed by architect George Vernon Russell, they were not disappointed.

The interior was lavishly appointed in Baroque style á la Hollywood, with heavy green silk drapery along the walls and a ceiling painted the unlikely shade of American Beauty red. Wall sofas of silk had been dyed to match the ceiling. The bandstand was flanked by bronze columns and urns that had been wired as lighting fixtures, and Emil Coleman's orchestra did the honors for the two consecutive opening nights. *Almost* everybody in Hollywood turned up in response to the advance publicity, and Ciro's was an overnight success that went on for several decades. It immediately became a sought-after location for post-premiere parties, birthday celebrations and other events. A Los Angeles furrier hired it for a fashion show that could only have happened in Hollywood: the models who displayed his expensive wares were each accompanied by a live animal to match – leopards, beavers and minks got their first look at the local wildlife as they paraded the runway at Ciro's.

Along with the stars, of course, came Hedda and Louella to chronicle their doings and undoings. Veronica Lake's drinking problem became a matter of public record. Judy Garland's escorts were enumerated in excruciating detail. Handsome leading men were regularly ejected for fighting, adding to the club's reputation if not to their own. When leggy, blonde Lana Turner, a new screen goddess, proclaimed Ciro's her

Previous pages: Errol Flynn and Joan Blondell in an animated discussion at Romanoff's as Bruce Cabot looks on apprehensively.

Below: Gary Cooper (center) and his party enliven a table at Ciro's. On the left is Fred MacMurray, seated next to Mrs Cooper (back to camera). On the right are J Watson Webb and Mrs MacMurray.

favorite nightspot, traffic became even heavier. As was his wont, Wilkerson soon tired of his successful new enterprise and moved on down the road to establish La Rue, leaving Herman Hover in charge. The club's popularity did not diminish, although it went through several changes of management and decor in ensuing years.

Another entertainment venture of early 1940 was the opening of Casa Mañana – Frank Sebastian's old Cotton Club in a new incarnation as a modern dance ballroom. The town was feeling the lack of the Palomar, which had burned to the ground the previous year, fortunately without loss of life. Casa Mañana stepped into the gap and became a

favorite with big-name bands on tour. Skinnay Ennis opened the hall, and many popular performers would succeed him.

Many stars had loaned their names or financial backing to Hollywood night spots since the days of Fatty Arbuckle's Plantation, and the practice continued into the 1940s. Early in May, a consortium that included Bing Crosby, Bob Hope, Fred MacMurray, Johnny Weismuller, Ken Murray, Rudy Vallee, Tony Martin and Errol Flynn opened the Pirate's Den on LaBrea near Beverly, a site formerly occupied by the Three Little Pigs. It was all rather like a children's party on the Jolly Roger theme, with female patrons regularly 'abducted' by bands of roving

Below left: Basil Rathbone and Joan Fontaine seem to be enjoying the excitement at Hollywood's newest watering hole, Ciro's.

Below: The irrepressible Bob Hope appears at a 'Salvador Dali party' in Del Monte dressed as a bad dream. His companion is Mrs Lent Hooker.

pirates and thrown into the brig. Release was gained by screaming until the victim was awarded a 'scream diploma,' suitably inscribed. The Skull and Bones bar offered 'six mystifying drinks' and a view of mock battles staged by the costumed waiters, complete with subsequent 'hangings' and 'floggings.' 'Bodies' were disposed of in a wheelbarrow. (Later, during the war years, a bottle gallery featured mockups of Tojo, Hitler and Mussolini as the target for empty flagons.) If good taste was in abeyance, customers were not – the Pirate's Den rated 'Yo-ho-hos' from the movie crowd for years.

Producer and playwright Preston Sturges, whose first nightclub venture had been in partnership with Ted Snyder, launched out on his own in the summer of 1940 with a new concept - The Players', named for the actors' club on New York's Gramercy Park. The spacious building, in the villa style, was at the foot of the hills along Sunset Boulevard. Sturges's unusual admission policy was to close the club entirely when he wanted to entertain his personal friends; when the public did get in, a customer who merely looked undesirable was ejected without ceremony. Originally, the club was a two-level restaurant, but when it showed a loss –

not surprisingly – after the first season, Sturges changed his operation to include a music-and-dance venue called the Playroom, which opened early in 1942. Both writers and players made it a favorite hangout from the start, on the basis of excellent food in the Blue Room, good sounds and even a private barber shop on the mezzanine. The new Players' found favor with Howard Hughes, Barbara Stanwyck, Orson Welles, Humphrey Bogart and many other regulars.

A new contender for the mantle of the Palomar arose in the form of the Palladium, which had its opening on Halloween night, 1940. Sunset Boulevard was thronged with would-be entrants to the new million-dollar ballroom, which the columnists described glowingly as Super Ballroom and Everybody's Night Club. Frank Don Riha, who had decorated Earl Carroll's, had outdone himself here. A kidney-shaped dance floor cushioned with cork provided 12,000 square feet of space for 7500 dancers, who could be viewed from the balcony that circled the entire room. Wide, sweeping staircases were flanked by dancing female figures. The color scheme was silver and pearl grey with coral accents, and huge lucite panels etched with more elegant female forms dominated the bandstand area. The college crowd was wooed with a 200-foot milk bar finished in emerald green, and Riha's specially designed 'Color Symphonies' consisted of lighting syncopated to the music - from blues and orchids for waltzes to bright red for rhumbas. Tommy Dorsey blew the opening note on his inimitable trombone, and Dorothy Lamour cut the symbolic orchid-draped ribbon. It was estimated that 10,000 people jammed the capacious building for the great event, while hundreds more surged outside for a glimpse of the latest arrivals. The sterling array of talent on display that opening night was soon followed by Kay Kyser, Artie Shaw, Glen Miller, Larry Clinton, Glen Gray and Frank Sinatra. The word was out: the Palladium was America's new showplace par excellence. During Glen Miller's appearance, six months after the opening, the audience was a who's who of established and up-and-coming stars including Bing Crosby, Bob Hope, Alice Faye, Betty Grable, George Raft, Lana Turner, Judy Garland, Rudy Vallee, the Andrews Sisters and Abbott and Costello.

The new Ciro's and Palladium-style night life signaled a turn away from the loud, frenetic, sometimes illegal action offered at places like the Clover Club and even the Troc. A series of raids in 1940 hindered their operations, and the underworld element represented by men like Bugsy Siegel and Farmer Page found it increasingly difficult to do their kind of business in reform-minded Los Angeles. They were moving to Nevada, where gambling was out in the open, and their gun-toting guards and bouncers went with them. The new clubs were more elegant and refined, toned down to a level that had become more acceptable to their patrons, many of whom had taken to staying at home nights during the late 1930s.

One of Hollywood's most colorful and legendary figures emerged in 1940: Michael Romanoff, who alleged that he was, among other things, 'the cousin of the late tsar of all the Russias. 'The Emperor,' as his numerous friends referred to him, managed to raise enough money from movie people including Cary Grant, Robert Benchley and Darryl Zanuck, to open his own restaurant on stylish Rodeo Drive in Beverly Hills. The menu was adorned with a regal portrait of Prince Mike himself, and the unlikely wallpaper (green, orange and yellow) was the proprietor's personal choice. An eclectic array of decorations was borrowed from various friends, and the layout was conducive to conversational groupings. Romanoff's offered top-quality food and privacy – tourists, autograph hounds and unknowns got short shrift. Exclusivity was fostered by the practice of reserving the first seven banquettes on the

left, opposite the bar, for stockholders and regulars, including Humphrey Bogart, who dined at Romanoff's almost daily. The host mingled freely with his guests, but usually dined alone, often with his two bulldogs, Socrates and Confucius (who were seated at the table). All of this appealed to Hollywood's endless quest for novelty, and Romanoff's became known all over the country as a citadel of low-key sophistication. Regulars idled the entire day away playing gin rummy and backgammon.

Above: Romanoff's Restaurant quickly became a byword for sophisticated socializing after its opening on Rodeo Drive in 1940. 'Prince Mike' protected the privacy of his guests by barring tourists, reporters and autograph seekers.

Left: Tommy Dorsey's band headlined at the Hollywood Palladium three weeks after Pearl Harbor.

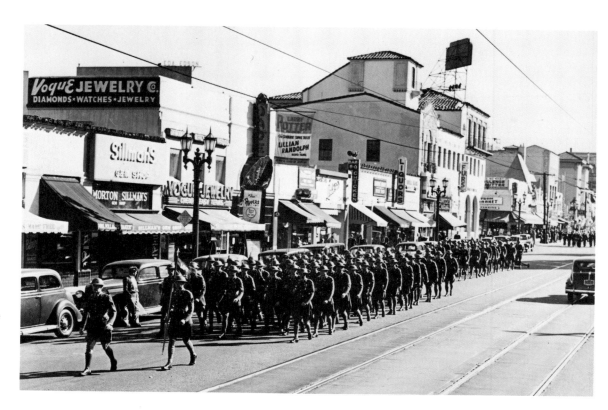

Right: An infantry company marches down Hollywood Boulevard.

Below: Wallace Beery reports for duty in the US Navy.

The year's end saw a burst of anticipation about another opening, scheduled for New Year's but put off until 3 January 1941, when Mocambo made its bow on Sunset Strip. A steady stream of first-nighters made their eager entry into the extraordinary setting provided by owners Felix Young and former agent Charlie Morrison. It was described as 'a cross between a somewhat decadent Imperial Rome, Salvador Dali, and a birdcage.' The nightclub's Mexican name had little to do with the decor, which included bright red columns ornamented with harlequins, rows of ball fringe hanging from lacquered trees and a dizzying blend of stripes, silver and huge tin flowers. Most striking of all was an aviary of live birds, including 21 parakeets, 4 love birds, 4 macaws, and a cockatoo. Local animal lovers got word of these ornamental captives before the opening and became incensed, fearing that the birds would be disturbed by the noise level of the club, but Morrison convinced the authorities that the birds would be having even more fun that the patrons. He also promised to keep the drapes drawn all day to allow them plenty of rest. These assurances given, Mocambo was allowed to open on schedule and the owners' $100,000 investment was secure.

Despite – or because of – these bizarre features, Mocambo was an immediate hit. Even homebodies, and competitors like Mike Romanoff, turned out to sample the good food and good times. The immensely popular Ciro's had a rival, and the two clubs would set the pace throughout the war years. Mocambo lured Phil Ohman and his band away from the Trocadero and imported the long-time maitre 'd at "21," Andre, from New York. Continental chef August Roche presided over the kitchen with an iron hand. As fan-magazine reporter Lloyd Pantages observed, 'Mocambo is a place in Hollywood which looks like Hollywood – magnificent, luxurious, exotic and unique.' Romanoff's and the Cocoanut Grove remained popular, but except for the new Palladium and Earl Carroll's, most of the early 1940s nightclubs were more subdued and sophisticated than those of the two previous decades. Loud bands, fights and aggressive novelties were going out of style.

Another feature of the prewar years was the emergence of black talent and entertainment along Central Avenue – Hollywood's answer to Harlem – and in other parts of town. On Sunset Boulevard, Little Eva replaced the former Baghdad nightclub with a domed dining and dancing hall that offered Southern cooking and entertainment in a decor dominated by scenes from *Uncle Tom's Cabin* and Mississippi riverboat days. Billie Holiday drew crowds to Cafe Society in the San Fernando Valley in the fall of 1941. 'Colored Revues' headlined at the Bal Tabarin in Gardena and the Stork Club on Western, but Central Avenue was the real stronghold of black talent on the West Coast. The Dunbar Hotel, the Last Word and the Club Alabam were at the heart of the action, offering entertainers on the order of Duke Ellington and Cab Calloway, plus chorus lines, floor shows and orchestras. In Compton, 'California's largest Harlem nightclub,' the Plantation, showcased the talents of visiting New York celebrities. Spirited jam sessions and spontaneous dance routines here often outshone the watered-down 'Sepia' revues staged in Hollywood and Los Angeles proper.

During these first two years of the new decade, Hollywood had taken uneasy notice of the war in Europe in such films as Alexander Korda's *That Hamilton Woman* (1941) and Chaplin's brilliant and controversial *The Great Dictator* (1940). Alfred Hitchcock, newly arrived from England, angered isolationists with his provocative *Foreign Correspondent* (1940), which implicitly demanded that America take a stand in the struggle against totalitarianism. Darker visions that would seem increasingly prophetic as the grim decade wore on appeared in *Citizen Kane* and *The Maltese Falcon* (1941). For the most part, though, 1940-41 brought movie business as usual: screwball and sophisticated comedies, melodrama and swashbucklers starring Errol Flynn and Tyrone Power. Until year's end, when the Japanese attack on Pearl Harbor, Hawaii, plunged the United States into the war.

The shockwaves reverberated from the far-off islands to the capitals of the world, mobilizing the nation almost overnight, and with it, Hollywood. The studios geared up to produce patriotic war films, the stars signed up for bond drives and the old nightclub known as The Barn, on Cahuenga near Sunset, was renovated into the famous Hollywood Canteen with the help of funds donated by Ciro's and Columbia Studios. War workers and servicemen jammed the Los Angeles area, and the lights went back on in the clubs and restaurants that had darkened after 7 December. The entertainment capital of the world mobilized all its resources of money, talent and technology to 'put on a show' that would bolster morale around the world. Many of Hollywood's brightest names donned uniforms and went into action; others risked their lives to raise money for the war effort, or to bring entertainment to troops on foreign battlefields. Hollywood, like all the world, had gone to war. It, too, would never be the same again.

Below: Still swinging despite the war, Joan Crawford, an accomplished dancer, joins an impromptu jitterbug contest during a break in the filming of *They All Kissed the Bride* (1942).

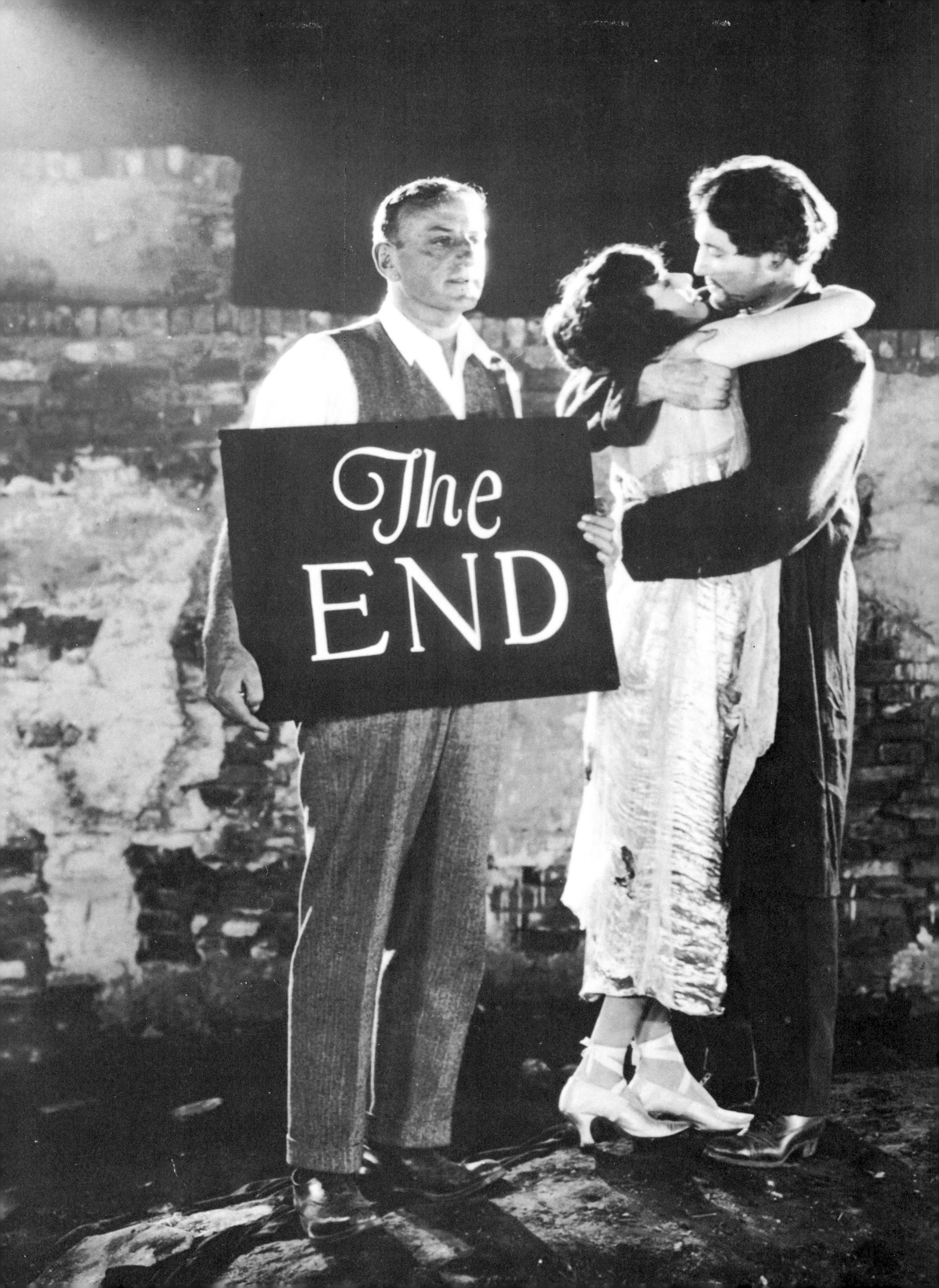
The END

INDEX

Acknowledgments

The author and publisher would like to thank the following people who have helped in the production of this book: Elizabeth Miles Montgomery, the editor; David Eldred, the designer; Jean Chiaramonte Martin who carried out the picture research, and Florence Norton, who prepared the index.

Picture Credits

AMPAS: pages 25 (bottom), 35, 37 (top), 38, 44, 72 (top), 178 (top).
The Bettmann Archive Inc: pages 1, 8 (top), 10 (bottom), 11 (bottom), 13 (top and bottom right), 24 (right), 25 (top left), 27 (bottom), 30 (bottom), 31, 32, 36 (bottom), 39, 54 (top), 55 (both), 56 (both), 58, 67 (top), 68 (top), 71, 76 (top), 77 (top), 78, 80 (bottom), 86 (left), 87 (bottom), 89 (both), 90 (left), 91 (top), 93, 96 (both), 102, 103 (all three), 104, 106 (all four), 113 (both), 115, 116 (both), 117, 119 (both), 127 (bottom), 128 (both), 129 (both), 130

(both), 132 (bottom), 133, 136 (top), 143, 146 (bottom), 149 (both), 150-1, 152-3, 153 (bottom), 154 (bottom), 155 (both), 156 (both), 157 (both), 158, 159 (bottom), 160, 161 (both), 162 (both), 163, 165 (both), 166, 167 (top), 169 (all three), 170, 172 (bottom), 173 (both), 174, 175 (bottom right), 176, 179, 180-1, 187, 188-9.
Bison Picture Library: pages 114 (bottom), 168, 172 (top).
Cal Poly State University, Special Collections: pages 144, 145, 146 (top).
California Department of Parks and Recreation, Office of Public Relations: page 108 (bottom).
Hearst San Simeon State Historical Monument, California Department of Parks and Recreation: pages 107 (bottom), 108 (top), 109, 147 (bottom).
Jim Heimann: pages 19, 57 (all three), 66 (bottom), 77 (bottom), 94 (bottom), 97 (top), 98 (all four), 99, (top, right, bottom), 112 (all five), 185 (bottom).

Larry Edmunds Book Shop: pages 92 (all four), 100-01 (all eight).
Library of Congress: page 105.
Museum of Modern Art/Film Stills Archive: pages 23 (top), 33 (top), 153 (top).
National Film Archive, London: page 30 (top).
Phototeque: pages 9 (bottom), 10 (top), 12 (top), 14 (both), 15, 20-1, 22 (top), 25 (top right), 26 (both), 27 (top), 28 (top), 29 (top), 33 (bottom), 36 (top), 37 (bottom), 40 (both), 41, 42 (both), 43, 45 (bottom), 54 (bottom), 59 (bottom), 60-1, 62, 63 (bottom), 68 (bottom), 69 (top), 72 (bottom), 73 (bottom), 75 (bottom), 79 (bottom), 81 (both), 82 (top), 86 (right), 87 (top), 88 (both), 90 (right), 91 (bottom), 94 (top), 95, 110-11, 135 (top), 142 (both), 147 (top), 152, 159 (top), 171 (both), 175 (top), 182, 183 (bottom left), 186 (bottom).
Schomberg Center for Research in Black Culture, New York Public Library: page 49 (top).
UPI/Bettmann Newsphotos: pages 13 (bottom left), 24 (left), 118, 122

(both), 123 (bottom), 124 (top), 134 (bottom), 186 (top).
Marc Wanamaker/Bison Archives: pages 2-3, 4-5, 6-7, 8 (bottom), 9 (top), 11 (top), 12 (bottom), 16 (both), 17, 18-19, 20 (bottom), 23 (bottom), 28 (bottom), 29 (bottom), 34, 45 (top), 48, 50 (both), 52 (bottom), 53 (both), 59 (top), 64 (both), 65 (both), 67 (bottom), 69 (bottom), 70, 76 (bottom), 79 (top), 82 (bottom), 83, 84-5, 99 (left), 107 (top four), 110 (top two), 111 (top two), 114 (top), 115 (top), 120-1, 123 (top), 124 (bottom), 125 (both), 126 (both), 127 (top), 131, 132 (top), 134 (top), 135 (bottom), 136 (bottom), 137, 138 (all three), 139 (all three), 140 (both), 141 (both), 142 (top), 148 (both), 154 (top), 164, 167 (top), 175 (bottom left), 177, 178 (bottom), 183 (top and bottom right), 185 (top).
Whittington Collection/California State University at Long Beach Special Collections: pages 46-7, 49 (bottom), 51 (both), 52 (top), 63 (top), 66 (bottom), 73 (top), 74, 75 (top), 80 (top), 184.